Confessing Christ

CALVIN K. CUMMINGS

GREAT COMMISSION PUBLICATIONS

Scripture quotations taken from the HOLY BIBLE,
NEW INTERNATIONAL VERSION. Copyright © 1973, 1978, 1984,
International Bible Society.

ISBN 0-934688-04-4

First printing 1955
Revised 1963
Revised 1977
Seventh printing 1990
Revised 1992

Printed in USA

Published by Great Commission Publications

Business office
7001 Peachtree Industrial Blvd., Suite 120
Norcross, GA 30092-3652

Editorial office
1250 Easton Road, Suite 160
Horsham, PA 19044-1409

TABLE OF CONTENTS

PREFACE

This booklet is designed for use in communicant church membership classes. Only the barest essentials are included. You may want to supplement each chapter with material of your own. You must be careful, however, not to make the course too extensive. The course is designed simply as a primer in the Christian faith from a biblical, Reformed perspective.

The class will get the maximum benefit by using the review section and discussion questions at the end of each chapter. The review should help the student recall, clarify and clinch the truths presented. The discussion questions will stimulate the student to reflect on and search the Scriptures, leading to a deeper understanding and appreciation of the truth.

These lessons can be presented in seven to thirteen one-hour periods, depending on the amount of supplementary material used and the extent of the discussions.

Our father, author Calvin K. Cummings, Sr., went to be with the Savior he faithfully confessed in December, 1987. It is with love and appreciation for him that we have revised *Confessing Christ* at the request of our mother. We have made use of our father's own class notes and followed his pattern for addressing new issues and needs in the church and making fresh application of biblical truth. Additional Scripture references and support have also been included. The revision holds precisely to the doctrinal standpoint of the first three editions, yet this revision is needed to assist pastors in sending forth this same truth into a less biblically literate and more diverse world. There is no longer the common knowledge of the Bible that there was before Bible reading was taken out of our public schools. The revision assumes less knowledge of Scripture by the reader, yet builds on the original body of content to lead people to the same place—a life that confesses Christ.

It is our prayer that *Confessing Christ* may continue to be used to reach men and women for the Savior and solidly build his church.

A leader's guide to *Confessing Christ* is now available that includes suggestions on how to teach each lesson. It also contains a helpful section by the author for pastors on "How to Conduct an Instruction Class for Prospective Church Members."

Our special thanks to Mrs. Dorothy Wright who, first having been ministered to by *Confessing Christ*, gave herself in loving and persevering ministry to type this revision.

Wilson L. Cummings
Calvin K. Cummings, Jr.
David B. Cummings

INTRODUCTION

WHAT DOES IT REALLY MEAN TO BE A CHRISTIAN? What is involved in making a public confession of faith in Christ as Savior and Lord and uniting with his church? This brief series of studies addresses these and other questions.

Your relationship to Jesus Christ is the most important question of all. Eternal salvation depends upon accepting and confessing Christ. The apostle Paul wrote: "If you confess with your mouth, 'Jesus is Lord,' and believe in your heart that God raised him from the dead, you will be saved. For it is with your heart that you believe and are justified, and it is with your mouth that you confess and are saved" (Romans 10:9, 10). Christ said, "Therefore whoever confesses me before men, him I will also confess before my Father who is in heaven. But whoever denies me before men, him I will also deny before my Father who is in heaven" (Matthew 10:32, 33—NKJV).

But what does it mean to confess Christ? What is involved in confessing faith in Christ publicly? These questions will be addressed in these lessons. The goal is that you will make a good confession of faith in Christ to the glory of God and your eternal happiness.

1

THE BIBLE

The Basis of Our Confession

We come to know our friends and family by listening to them. Through listening we grow to understand who they are and what they are like. The same is true of Christ. To confess Christ we must first know Christ. We come to know Christ only by listening to God communicate to us in the Bible. If we refuse to read the Bible or to accept the Bible as altogether trustworthy, we can never really know and confess Christ; he is forever lost to us. It is absolutely essential, therefore, that we know just what the Bible is and why it is important. The Bible is the very foundation of Christianity. Upon that foundation depends our eternal destiny. We must therefore carefully examine this foundation of the Christian faith and life—the Bible.

The Word of God

The word *Bible* means "book." It is called the "holy" Bible because it is set apart from all other books as sacred. It is commonly called the "Word of God." But what do we mean by calling the Bible "God's Word"? We mean that God is the author; the word that he speaks is *his* word. Just as your word is what comes from you, so God's Word is the word that comes from him. The creeds of Christianity all confess that the Bible is "inspired" and "infallible." The word *inspired* means "God-breathed." When we say that the Bible is inspired, we mean that God breathed into the writers of Scripture his thoughts and words. What they wrote was not merely a product of their own minds and hearts; they wrote God's thoughts and words as revealed to them by God's Holy Spirit. Thus the Bible is infallible. The original writings as recorded in Hebrew and in Greek are free from all error; every word as well as every thought is true.

How Do We Know?

But how can we know that the Bible is the inspired and infallible Word of God? That is the all-important question.

Some say that we know the Bible is the Word of God because the church made the Bible, and the church is infallible. But what is the church? The church is made up of sinful, fallible human beings like you and me. To base our confidence in the Bible upon a statement of the church is to build our faith upon the quicksands of mere human authority. The Bible is thus said to be the Word of God because *we* say so: the mind of man becomes the final standard of truth. Yet man is so obviously full of contradiction, confusion, error and sin that to build our faith on a foundation of human opinion is to invite disaster.

Bible-believing Christians believe the Bible is the Word of God on the authority not of man but of God. God in his Word claims to be its author. He provides evidence in the Bible that it is indeed the very Word of God. He gives us his Holy Spirit, who shows us his hand and voice in all of Holy Scripture. We build our faith on the solid rock of God himself. We rest upon divine revelation, not human reason, as the foundation for our faith in the Bible as God's Word. Since this revelation is the very foundation of our Christian faith, we will look at three ways God testifies that the Bible is his Word.

1. God in His Word Claims to Be Its Author

Every letter we receive has a signature This signature tells us who the author is. The same is true of the Bible. It has God's signature.

This signature is not in some little space at the end of the Bible, as in letters. God's signature is written all over the Scriptures, from beginning to end. Throughout the Bible, God testifies time and again that he, not man, is speaking and writing. In the Old Testament alone, the expression "thus says the Lord" or its equivalent occurs some 2,000 times. The sacred name of God is brought forward to compel the whole world to hear and obey his word.

The most significant testimony in Scripture to its own inspiration and infallibility is the witness of Christ, the Son of God. Christ, the second person of the Trinity, regarded the Scriptures of the Old Testament in their entirety as the word of God. He promised that the same Holy Spirit who inspired the writers of the Old Testament would inspire the writers of the New Testament. What did Jesus really believe and teach about the Bible?

Jesus believed and taught unmistakably that the Scriptures of the Old Testament are the final, authoritative and infallible Word of God. Three times he was tempted by Satan in the wilderness (Matthew 4:3–10), and each time he appealed to the infallible authority of Scripture. 1) When tempted to turn stones into bread, he replied, "It is written: 'Man does not live on bread alone, but on every word that comes from the mouth of God.' " 2) When Satan dared Christ to tempt God by leaping off the pinnacle of the temple, Christ said, "It is also written: 'Do not put the Lord your God to the test.' " 3) When Satan offered Christ the kingdoms of the world if he would only fall down and worship him, Christ answered, "Away from me, Satan! For it is written: 'Worship the Lord your God, and serve him only.' "

Each time, Christ rebuffed Satan with the words "It is written." And he expects us to do the same. He appeals to the Scriptures of the Old Testament as being that final Word. He says, in effect, "Satan, I cannot do these things; they are contrary to the Bible. The written Word of God is my infallible rule of faith and conduct."

This same attitude toward the Old Testament Scriptures is reflected in other teachings of Jesus. In his Sermon on the Mount, Christ said, "Do not think that I have come to abolish the Law or the Prophets; I have not come to abolish them but to fulfill them. I tell you the truth, until heaven and earth disappear, not the smallest letter, not the least stroke of a pen, will by any means disappear from the Law until everything is accomplished" (Matthew 5:17, 18).

On another occasion, in answering his critics Jesus quoted from one of the psalms and added, "The Scripture cannot be broken" (John 10:35). When Peter tried to prevent Christ's death, Christ appealed to the prophecies of the Old Testament: "But how then would the Scriptures be fulfilled that say it must happen in this way?" (Matthew 26:54). These quotations affirm that Jesus regarded the Law, the Psalms and the Prophets as unalterably true. The Law, the Psalms and the Prophets together make up the entire Old

Testament. Jesus thus accepted the whole Old Testament as God's Word.

But what about the New Testament? The New Testament had not yet been written when Christ was on earth. How then can we appeal to Christ's authority for the New Testament's inspiration?

Christ promised that the same Holy Spirit who inspired the authors of the Old Testament would be given to those who would write the books of the New Testament. He promised his apostles: "But when he, the Spirit of truth, comes, he will guide you into all truth. He will not speak on his own; he will speak only what he hears, and he will tell you what is yet to come" (John 16:13). He also gave his apostles the authority to act and speak in his name: "I will give you the keys of the kingdom of heaven; whatever you bind on earth will be bound in heaven, and whatever you loose on earth will be loosed in heaven" (Matthew 16:19). Both Protestant and Roman Catholic scholars agree that each of the 27 books of the New Testament was either written or approved by an apostle. The New Testament, then, comes to us as the Word of God upon the authority of Jesus Christ, God's Son.

The apostles of our Lord, endowed with the promise of the Spirit and divine authority, give some of the clearest statements concerning the Scriptures. Paul, writing of the Old Testament Scriptures, declared, "All Scripture is God-breathed" (2 Timothy 3:16). Peter wrote, "For prophecy never had its origin in the will of man, but men spoke from God as they were carried along by the Holy Spirit" (2 Peter 1:21).

Referring to his own message, which makes up about one-half of the New Testament, Paul affirmed: "When you received the word of God, which you heard from us, you accepted it not as the word of men, but as it actually is, the word of God" (1 Thessalonians 2:13). Peter places Paul's letters in the same class as the writings of the Old Testament: "…just as our dear brother Paul also wrote you with the wisdom that God gave him. He writes the same way in all his letters.…His letters contain some things that are hard to understand, which ignorant and unstable people distort, as they do the other Scriptures, to their own destruction" (2 Peter 3:15, 16). Paul referred to Luke's Gospel as Scripture. Quoting from Luke 10:7, he wrote: "For the Scripture says…'The worker deserves his wages' " (1 Timothy 5:18).

Only one conclusion is left: "The authority of the holy Scripture, for which it ought to be believed, and obeyed, dependeth not upon the testimony of any man, or church; but wholly upon God (who is truth itself) the author thereof: and therefore it is to be received, because it is the Word of God" (Westminster Confession of Faith, chap. 1, sec. 4—hereafter WCF, chap. 1, sec. 4). We are dependent creatures. The only way that we can think is to base our opinions upon some authority. If you do not base your thinking on God and his Word, then you will base it upon limited human reason, and something else will have become your final authority.

There is no better reason to believe the Bible is the Word of God than because God himself says so. What if you approached God and asked him why you should believe the Bible was his Word, and he said, "I'm sorry, you will have to consult the experts for the reasons."? Then God has passed the buck and is no longer God. He is no longer the ultimate authority.

But God is the only one who knows everything. He is therefore the only ultimate authority to be trusted. We are limited and sinful. We can never be certain about anything unless the One who is holy and all-knowing reveals it to us. If God was not all-knowing, there would be room for doubt. What is discovered tomorrow might contradict what God says in the Bible today. But God is all-knowing; nothing will be discovered tomorrow that will contradict what he says today. God took into account all past and future discoveries and eventualities when he declared his will in his Word. God's Word and God's claims about his Word can always be counted on. "Cursed is the one who trusts in man….But blessed is the man who trusts in the Lord" (Jeremiah 17:5, 7).

2. The Evidence within Scripture Confirms the Claim That the Bible Is God's Word

The Bible not only has God's signature; it has the evidence within to confirm the claim that it is God's Word.

An illustration may be useful here. Suppose you received a letter signed by the President of the United States. But the stationery lacks the official letterhead, the postmark is of a place you never heard of, the style is crude and the contents insignificant. You would be right to conclude that the letter was a fake. It could not have been written by the President, residing in the capital, whose interests are political and whose style has authority.

God not only makes the claim that the Bible is his Word; he makes good his claim. He provides within the Holy Scriptures abundant evidence to support that claim. The Westminster Confession says it best: "The heavenliness of the matter, the efficacy of the doctrine, the majesty of the style, the consent of all the parts, the scope of the whole (which is, to give all glory to God), the full discovery it makes of the only way of man's salvation, the many other incomparable excellencies, and the entire perfection thereof, are arguments whereby it doth abundantly evidence itself to be the Word of God" (WCF, chap. 1, sec. 5).

Consider the amazing harmony and the underlying *unity* of the sacred writings. The Bible is a compilation of 66 books written by 36 different authors over a period of 1,600 years. The authors did not sit down as a committee to decide what to write. They were separated by great time and distance. Yet their books are marked by harmony, not confusion or contradiction. Amid diversity there is an underlying unity. The Old Testament points forward to the Savior to come. The New Testament tells of the Savior who has come: "And beginning with Moses and all the Prophets, he [Christ] explained to them what was said in all the Scriptures concerning himself" (Luke 24:27). Only one reasonable explanation exists for this marvelous unity—there was one mind that conceived the plan, one hand that wrote the words: the mind and hand of God.

One of the most remarkable evidences of God's divine authorship of the Scriptures is the prophecies of the Old Testament fulfilled in the New Testament. Eight hundred years before the birth of Christ the prophets declared that Christ would be born, how he would be born, where he would be born, what kind of person he would be and what kind of work he would perform. Listen as the prophets speak: "The virgin will be with child and will give birth to a son, and will call him Immanuel [God with us]" (Isaiah 7:14). "But you, Bethlehem Ephrathah, though you are small among the clans of Judah, out of you will come for me one who will be ruler over Israel, whose origins are from of old, from ancient times" (Micah 5:2). "And he will be called Wonderful Counselor, Mighty God, Everlasting Father, Prince of Peace" (Isaiah 9:6). "But he was pierced for our transgressions, he was crushed for our iniquities; the punishment that brought us peace was upon him, and by his wounds we are healed. We all, like sheep, have gone astray, each of us has turned to his own way; and the Lord has laid on him the iniquity of us all" (Isaiah 53:5, 6).

The New Testament records the fulfillment of all these prophecies. No one can accurately predict what a year, or even a day, will bring forth. But these prophets of old peer through the ages and tell in graphic detail of the Coming One. There is only one satisfactory explanation. The Spirit of the Lord was upon them; they saw the future unveiled as only the Divine Architect of the universe could uncover it.

The *basic message* of the Bible also provides evidence to convince us that the authors were not writing their own thoughts but God's thoughts. What is the central message of the Bible? It is the story of man's complete ruin in sin, of his inability to save himself, and of the power of God's grace alone to save him. This is a humbling message that the human mind would not naturally think up. When left to himself, man has always invented another kind of religion. All human religions teach that man is not completely sinful and that he can somehow, in some way, save himself. The Bible teaches that man is dead in sin, cannot save himself, and can be saved only by the grace of God. This is contrary to the proud thoughts of the natural man. We don't naturally, in humility, admit our failures and inability. To teach about our sin and need for salvation is evidence that the authors of the Bible were controlled not by their own spirits but by God's Holy Spirit (2 Peter 1:21).

This evidence within Scripture confirms its divine origin. There is external evidence in *archaeology* and *history* that also confirms its truthfulness. This is a fascinating and faith-strengthening study that we cannot present here.

There is, however, one other testimony to the complete trustworthiness of the Scriptures: the witness of God the Holy Spirit in the heart of the believer.

3. The Testimony of God's Holy Spirit in Our Hearts

How can some read the claims of Scripture to be the Word of God and study the evidence for such claims, only to reject the Bible as inspired of God? Others read and believe with an unshakable conviction that the Bible is God's inspired Word. The difference is not from lack of evidence (John 20:30, 31; Luke 16:31). The difference is that some have not been given the Holy Spirit to enable them to see the truth of the Bible's claims. They are spiritually blind and prejudiced; they cannot see the truth. They are spiritually dead; they cannot hear the voice of God speaking in every line.

But just as the eye of the artist sees the beauty of the setting sun, the Holy Spirit enables the believer to see the hand of God in the Bible. There is only one God, yet this one God exists in three persons: the Father, the Son and the Holy Spirit. Just as your own spirit knows you better than others know you, the Holy Spirit knows God completely and is able to make God known. Just as the ear of the musician detects the genius of the composer in a symphony, the Spirit enables the believer to detect the genius of heaven in Holy Scripture. "However," declares Paul, "as it is written: 'No eye has seen, no ear has heard, no mind has conceived what God has prepared for those who love him'—but God has revealed it to us by his Spirit....We have not received the spirit of the world but the Spirit who is from God, that we may understand what God has freely given us" (1 Corinthians 2:9, 10, 12).

We need, then, to pray for the help of God's Holy Spirit as we read the Bible.

Review Questions

1. ˙How can we know Christ?

2. What do we mean when we speak of the Bible as "the Word of God"?

16

3. What do we mean when we say that the Bible is "inspired"?

4. What does the word *infallible* mean?

5. Should we believe in the Bible as God's Word because the church says so? Why or why not?

6. Why should we believe in the Bible as God's Word? How does this assure certainty?

7. What evidence supports the Bible's claim that it is God's Word?

8. Did Jesus accept the Bible as God's Word? If so, how?

9. In what ways did the apostles teach that the Bible is God's Word?

10. What evidence is there within the Bible that God is its author?

11. If a person does not believe that the Bible is God's Word, is it because there is not enough evidence?

12. Who gives the Christian the assurance in his heart that the Bible is the Word of God?

MEMORY WORK
2 Timothy 3:16, 17

All Scripture is God-breathed and is useful for teaching, rebuking, correcting and training in righteousness, so that the man of God may be thoroughly equipped for every good work. (NIV)

All Scripture is given by inspiration of God, and is profitable for doctrine, for reproof, for correction, for instruction in righteousness, that the man of God may be complete, thoroughly equipped for every good work. (NKJV)

Questions for Discussion

1. How would you answer a person who says, "I believe in Christ; and I believe in the Bible, but I don't believe it fits my situation."? (2 Timothy 3:14–17)

2. Is there anything wrong with our reasoning when we say the Bible is God's Word because the Bible says so?

3. What is the difference between saying that the *thoughts* of the Bible are true or that the Bible *contains* the word of God—and believing that every *word* of the Bible is the word of God? Which agrees with the evidence of Scripture itself? (Psalm 119:160)

4. What does the Westminster Confession of Faith teach concerning the inspiration of the Scriptures?

5. How would you respond to someone who says there are contradictions in the Bible?

6. Why weren't the books of the Apocrypha included in the Roman Catholic Bible until the Council of Trent in 1545–1563?

7. In what way do people and religions add extra revelation to the Bible? What is wrong with this? (Revelation 22:18, 19)

8. What difference does it make in our lives whether the Bible is the Word of God or not? (Matthew 7:24–27)

2

CHRIST

The One We Confess

The Bible is essentially God's revelation of himself. God is the eternal Creator who is infinitely higher than we are. Yet in great mercy he makes himself known to us (Isaiah 40:25–28). God's revelation of himself comes to its highest expression in Jesus Christ. Because God is a Spirit, "no one has ever seen God, but God the One and Only, who is at the Father's side, has made him known" (John 1:18). To know what God is, we must look at Jesus Christ. The apostle Paul wrote that we are given "the light of the knowledge of the glory of God in the face of Christ." (2 Corinthians 4:6).

The Old Testament reveals the shadows of Christ. The New Testament reveals Christ come in human flesh. Christ himself affirmed of the Old Testament Scriptures, "These are the Scriptures that testify about me" (John 5:39). The apostle John gives as his whole purpose in writing the Fourth Gospel: "These are written that you may believe that Jesus is the Christ, the Son of God, and that by believing you may have life in his name" (John 20:31).

Just who is this Jesus, and what did he come to do?

Who Is Jesus?

Some people will argue that it makes no difference what position we ascribe to Jesus as long as we follow his teachings. But that isn't what Jesus said. Jesus was deeply concerned to know the views people held about him. He asked the Pharisees of his day, "What do you think about the Christ? Whose son is he?" (Matthew 22:42). He asked his disciples, "Who do people say the Son of Man is?" (Matthew 16:13). He wanted to keep his status as God's chosen *Messiah* clearly in view.

Conflicting answers were given in Jesus' day as to who he was. Conflicting answers are still being given today. Turn to the Gospels and the Epistles of the New Testament to see what they really teach concerning Jesus of Nazareth. Whose son is he?

Jesus Christ is a fact. He entered history. Our calendar recognizes this fact by dividing all history into B.C. ("before Christ") and A.D. (*anno Domini*, "in the year of the Lord"). He was born a baby to the virgin Mary in a Bethlehem stable. He was like us in every way except one. He was "tempted in every way, just as we are—yet was without sin" (Hebrews 4:15). Jesus grew just as any other child grows. He grew mentally and physically, socially and spiritually. "And Jesus grew in wisdom and stature, and in favor with God and men" (Luke 2:52). He was tender and compassionate in his humanity. He shed tears at the tomb of his beloved friend Lazarus. He was moved with compassion toward the multitudes who were distressed like sheep without a shepherd.

But Jesus is more than a fact of history. He is unique. He is the grand supernatural fact of history. He was not just a child of time. He is timeless—the eternal Christ. He was the eternal God made visible in a human nature. The birth of Christ doesn't mark the time when Jesus came into existence. He always was. He said, "Before Abraham was born, I am!" (John 8:58). The birth of Christ simply means that he who always was took on a human nature. "In the beginning was the Word, and the Word was with God, and the Word was God....The Word became flesh and made his dwelling among us. We have seen his glory, the glory of the One and Only, who came from the Father, full of grace and truth" (John 1:1, 14). Jesus declared of himself, "I and the Father are one" (John 10:30). He boldly stated, "Anyone who has seen me has seen the Father" (John 14:9).

Christ testified under oath that he was the Son of God. He sealed that testimony with his blood. "Are you then the Son of God?" demanded the High Priest. He replied, "You are right in saying I am" (Luke 22:70). The apostle Paul sums up the teaching of the Scriptures concerning the person of Christ. "For in Christ all the fullness of the Deity [Godhead] lives in bodily form" (Colossians 2:9). In his resurrected body, Christ continues triumphantly today to be "God and man in two distinct natures, and one person, forever" (Westminster Shorter Catechism, Q/A 21—hereafter SC, Q/A 21).

How Can We Be Sure?

But how do we know that Jesus is God who has taken to himself human flesh? We know he is because the Bible tells us so. Remember, there is no higher authority or reason for believing in anything than the authority of God and his Word. There is no greater certainty than the Spirit's witness in our hearts. The Bible presents Jesus just as he really was and is. The true Christ is his own best evidence that he is all that he claimed to be. He was called to be a slave, the suffering servant. He is now transfigured in the glory of heaven, clothed in the royal robes of divine majesty. All that he is draws us to him, to trust him, to love and adore him. Look at Jesus as he comes to us in the Bible; observe just what it is that convinces us that he is fully God.

1. His Sinless Life

Louis Pasteur, the noted French scientist, once stated: "I would not know how to account for the life of Jesus if he were not the Son of God." The sinless life of Jesus is one of the most convincing proofs that he is God's only begotten Son. The life of Jesus is beyond reproach. No one can accuse him of wrong. His enemies tried. But their very accusations were tributes to his love and truthfulness. "He is a friend of tax collectors and sinners," they charged. They thus acknowledged his love for the unloved and unlovely. "He is guilty of blasphemy," they declared, and demanded his crucifixion. But as he died, the centurion exclaimed, "Surely this man was the Son of God!" Blasphemers don't pray for their enemies in the act of torturing and killing them, as Jesus did: "Father, forgive them, for they do not know what they are doing" (Luke 23:34).

2. His Supernatural Works

The miracles of Jesus are a further evidence of his deity. Some 33 of Jesus' miracles are recorded in the gospel narratives. They are woven into the very thread and fabric of his life. To separate the miracles from the life and teachings of Jesus is like trying to separate flesh from bones.

Thomas Jefferson tried to purge the New Testament of all miracles. He failed. "Go back and report to John what you hear and see: The blind receive sight, the lame walk, those who have leprosy are cured, the deaf hear, the dead are raised" (Matthew 11:4, 5). Thus Christ testified of his own works. Where did his power come from? No mere man could bring the dead back to life.

His miracles are proofs of the mighty power of God. They were intended to be. When some accusing bystanders questioned his right to forgive sins, Jesus confirmed his claim to be God by a miracle: " 'But that you may know that the Son of man has authority on earth to forgive sins….' He said to the paralytic, 'I tell you, get up, take your mat and go home.' He got up, took his mat and walked out in full view of them all" (Mark 2:10, 11, 12).

3. His Resurrection from the Dead

The crowning proof that Christ is the Son of the living God is his physical resurrection. The third day he rose from the dead with the same body that he took into the tomb. "Put your finger here; see my hands. Reach out your hand and put it into my side. Stop doubting and believe," Christ invited Thomas (John 20:27). "A ghost does not have flesh and bones, as you see I have" (Luke 24:39).

The empty tomb bears silent but eloquent testimony to the fact of the bodily resurrection of our Lord. On at least 12 different occasions Jesus appeared physically to witnesses. There is thus more evidence for the resurrection of Christ than for his birth. Only 2 narratives concern the birth of Christ. Twelve narratives deal with the resurrection appearances.

Added to this is compelling circumstantial evidence. A radical change occurred in the disciples. All except John had forsaken Christ before his crucifixion and fled like cowards. Peter even denied that he knew the Lord in order to save his own life. But suddenly there was a complete change in their conduct. With great boldness they began to testify of Christ. According to Christian tradition every apostle except John lost his life because he proclaimed Christ as risen from the dead. How do you account for such a sudden and complete change? There is only one satisfactory explanation: they saw the risen Christ.

What are the alternatives to accepting Christ as the Son of God? There are only two. One is to say that Christ was insane; he was deluded and deceived about himself. True, he was sincere: he really thought he was divine. Actually, however, he was fit only for a mental institution. But don't you see what happens when you try to make Jesus out to be insane—he who was the wisest man that ever lived? Who ends up being out of his mind?

The other alternative is to say with the Pharisees that Jesus is a devil, an impostor. He knew he wasn't God's Son; he deliberately deceived people. But when you try to make Jesus out to be devilish—he who has brought only good wherever he has been believed—who ends up being the devil? Instead, we must take Christ as he is and say in simple faith, "You are the Christ, the Son of the living God" (Matthew 16:16).

What Did Christ Come to Do?

The birth of Christ didn't just happen. Nothing in this God-planned universe just happens, least of all the coming of God's only begotten Son. God has a plan for this earth, a plan of salvation. From all eternity God purposed to save a people for himself. Christ came into the world for the salvation of those whom the Father had in love chosen to be his own.

Some hold that Christ's purpose was to teach; Christ, they say, was a master teacher, a great philosopher. He was certainly that. He was the greatest of teachers and philosophers. Others hold that his chief purpose was to show us how to live. And he is indeed our perfect example in all things. But Jesus regarded neither of these as his primary purpose in coming into the world. Christ came to be the Savior. The angel of the Lord announced at his birth, "You are to give him the name Jesus, because he will save his people from their sins" (Matthew 1:21). Jesus himself said, "For the Son of Man came to seek and to save what was lost" (Luke 19:10). He also declared, "The Son of Man did not come to be served, but to serve, and to give his life as a ransom for many" (Matthew 20:28).

To understand and appreciate this saving purpose for which Christ came into the world, we must first understand man's condition and destiny, and then God's character and purpose.

1. Man's Need

We are sinful, fallen creatures. "For all have sinned and fall short of the glory of God" (Romans 3:23). "As it is written: 'There is no one righteous, not even one' " (Romans 3:10). Sin is unspeakably horrible. It is breaking the law of God. Sin is rebellion against God; it is lawlessness. Unless we see ourselves in all our utter sinful misery we will never begin to understand why Christ came into the world. "Christ Jesus came into the world to save sinners—of whom I am the worst" (1 Timothy 1:15). That was Paul's testimony. It must also be our testimony if we are to know the Savior's grace. Do you think and say of yourself, "I'm not so bad," "I keep the Ten Commandments," "I live by the golden rule," or "I never hurt anybody"? Then you are far from the kingdom of God. Christ said, "I have not come to call the righteous, but sinners" (Matthew 9:13).

No one is farther from the kingdom of God than the self-righteous person. If this is you, then you need to pray fervently, "Lord, show me myself; show me myself as you see me." Then read Matthew 5:17–48; 22:37–40 and Romans 1:18–32; 3:10–18. Only when the Spirit of God causes you to cry out, "God, be merciful to me a sinner," can you be sure that God's grace has changed your heart.

Not only must you see your sin, you must also see that your sin has terrifying results. "For the wages of sin is death" (Romans 6:23). We are spiritually dead; we have no fellowship with the Father. Our future includes not only physical death but eternal death—eternal separation from the presence of the living God. "All mankind by their fall lost communion with God, are under his wrath and curse, and so made liable to all the miseries of this life, to death itself, and to the pains of hell forever" (SC, Q/A 19).

Christ, who spoke such tender words of grace, is the one who above all others warned of the terrors of hell: "Do not be afraid of those who kill the body but cannot kill the soul. Rather, be afraid of the One who can destroy both soul and body in hell" (Matthew 10:28). "Then will he say to those on his left, 'Depart from me, you who are cursed, into the eternal fire prepared for the devil and his angels' " (Matthew 25:41). These are the words of Christ, the Son of

God. They speak a tragic fact. But we must face it, not ignore it; accept it, not reject it. Only then will we have hope.

God speaks loving words of grace. But only when we admit our needy condition can we begin to appreciate the mysterious and matchless love of God in sending his Son to save us. Then the life and death of Christ for our salvation will have meaning for us, a truly glorious meaning.

2. God's Provision

To understand the meaning of Christ's coming we must also know that God is holy—infinitely, eternally and unchangeably holy. He cannot, he will not, treat sin lightly. His justice demands full punishment for sin. His holiness requires that the demands of the law be met in full. He would not be a God we could respect if he required anything less. Should we expect less justice from God than from a human judge? The earthly judge who lets a criminal go free without punishment is despised as unjust.

God is too pure to regard evil without executing justice. To know that the Lord is just should shake you to the very core of your being! But the same God who is strong in justice is also rich in mercy: "God is love" (1 John 4:8). In his eternal plan, God in love chose to redeem a people for himself as the object of his infinite and unchangeable love. Why he loved us, we will never know. This is the unfathomable mystery of God's divine grace. But that he loved us in Christ we can never doubt: "God demonstrates his own love for us in this: While we were still sinners, Christ died for us" (Romans 5:8).

The cross of Christ exhibits both the justice and the mercy of God. The basis of the cross is God's eternal justice; the spirit of the cross is God's eternal love. On the cross of Calvary, Christ suffered for the sins of his people. "Christ died for our sins according to the Scriptures" (1 Corinthians 15:3). As he instituted the Lord's Supper, Christ turned to his disciples and said: "This is my blood of the covenant, which is poured out for many for the forgiveness of sins" (Matthew 26:28).

Christ did two very important things for us. First, he died for us. The penalty for sin had to be paid, either by us or by someone else.

JUSTIFICATION BY FAITH

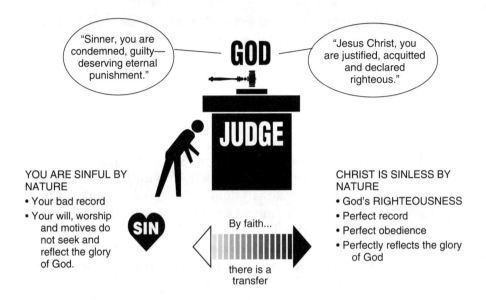

When you truly have faith in Jesus Christ, your sin is placed on Christ and Christ's righteousness is credited to your account.

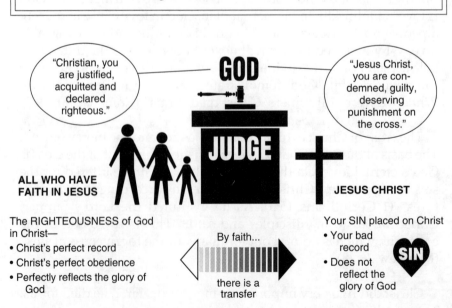

Jesus paid the penalty in full. He died in our place. He himself said that he came to "give his life as a ransom for [instead of] many" (Matthew 20:28). He was our substitute. He "loved me and gave himself for me," said Paul (Galatians 2:20).

Second, Christ lived for us; he obeyed the law in our place. Christ performed the perfect righteousness required by a holy God. "Be perfect, therefore, as your heavenly Father is perfect" (Matthew 5:48). But who of us is perfect? How can we sinners stand before a holy God? The answer is—through the perfect righteousness of Christ. As Paul wrote, "For just as through the disobedience of the one man [Adam] the many were made sinners, so also through the obedience of the one man [Christ] the many will be made righteous" (Romans 5:19); "not having a righteousness of my own that comes from the law, but that which is through faith in Christ—the righteousness that comes from God and is by faith" (Philippians 3:9). We are accepted as righteous in God's sight only for the righteousness of Christ credited to our account and received by faith alone.

When you have faith in Jesus Christ, not only did he die on the cross for your sin, but his righteousness is credited to your account. You are declared righteous in God's sight, not because of your own record, but because of Christ's perfect record credited to you (Romans 3:10–28; Philippians 3:4–9).

This great truth of justification by faith was rediscovered by the Protestant reformers. "Therefore, since we have been justified through faith, we have peace with God through our Lord Jesus Christ" (Romans 5:1). Do you have that peace? God sincerely and freely offers his grace to you. Have you found Christ as your Savior?

Review Questions (Part 1)

1. Who is God?

2. In whom does God's revelation of himself come to its highest expression?

3. Does it make any difference what position we ascribe to Jesus?

4. What is the evidence that Jesus was human?

6. In what three ways does Christ's life convince us that he is fully God?

7. Give some of the proof for the physical resurrection of Christ.

MEMORY WORK
Matthew 20:28

Just as the Son of Man did not come to be served, but to serve, and to give his life as a ransom for many. (NIV)

Just as the Son of Man did not come to be served, but to serve, and to give His life a ransom for many. (NKJV)

Questions for Discussion (Part 1)

1. What do we mean when we say that God is "Triune"? (Matthew 28:20)

2. Why is it important to believe Jesus was born of a virgin? (Luke 1:32–38)

3. How would you answer someone who said that Jesus' teachings are good, but he is not fully God?

4. If the evidence demonstrating that Jesus is God and Savior is clear, why do some reject him or treat him with indifference? (John 3:18–20)

Review Questions (Part 2)

1. What did Jesus say was his purpose in coming into the world?

2. Why do we need such a Savior? What kind of character does man have?

3. How do you define sin?

4. What does the Bible teach to be the consequences of sin?

5. Why can't God pass lightly over sin?

6. If we are sinful and God is just, how can you be saved? How can *anyone* be saved? *For help in answering this question, refer to the diagram on page 28 and Romans 3:21–28. You may also wish to look up Philippians 3:1–9.*

Questions for Discussion (Part 2)

1. How did we become sinners? (Genesis 1:26–31; 3:1–13)

2. If you would die tonight and appear before God, and he asked you, "Why should I let you into my Heaven?" what would you answer?

3. What excuse will God accept for your not being perfect? (Romans 3:19, 20)

4. What is the proof of God's love for sinners? (Romans 5:6–11)

5. For whom did Christ die? (John 10:11, 26–28; Ephesians 5:25; Acts 20:28; John 3:16–18)

3

REPENTANCE AND FAITH

Requirements of a True Confession

Does your heart move you to be a Christian? Would you really like to know and confess Jesus Christ as your very own Savior and Lord? Do you want to be at peace with God? Then you have to fulfill the requirements of a true confession of faith in Christ. The two basic elements of a true confession are repentance and faith. These are not two separate and distinct activities of a renewed person. You can't have the one without the other. If you truly repent of your sins, you will turn in faith to Christ. If you truly believe in Christ, you can't help but repent of your sins. Nor does one come before the other; they come together. But repentance should be considered first because it is the foundation for understanding the Bible's emphasis on the necessity and importance of faith.

Repentance

Repentance was the message of the Old Testament prophets and the message of John the Baptist. John preached repentance in order to prepare the way for the coming of Christ. Jesus himself attached such importance to repentance that he emphasized it in his very first recorded sermon: "The kingdom of God is near. Repent and believe the goodnews!" (Mark 1:15). He plainly said, "I have not come to call the righteous, but sinnners to repentance" (Luke 5:32). It is a *must:* "Unless you repent, you too will all perish" (Luke 13:3, 5).

What, then, is true repentance? "Repentance unto life is a saving grace, whereby a sinner, out of a true sense of his sin, and apprehension of the mercy of God in Christ, doth, with grief and hatred of his sin, turn from it unto God, with full purpose of, and endeavor after, new obedience" (SC, Q/A 87).

The primary word for repentance in the New Testament means a "change of heart or mind." Repentance is a change of heart granted by God. It includes a number of aspects.

1. Admission of Sin

The first aspect of repentance is the acknowledgment of sin. Your whole attitude toward sin must change. You must be convinced that you are a sinner. You can't admit your guilt if in your heart you really believe you are innocent. "Through the law we become conscious of sin" (Romans 3:20). The law of God requires—as Jesus reminded the Pharisees—that you "love the Lord your God with all your heart and with all your soul and with all your mind" and that you "love your neighbor as yourself" (Matthew 22:37, 39). No one does this. No one can.

We must admit our sin. We must swallow our pride and quit numbing our guilty consciences by making comforting comparisons with others. David said, "I know my transgressions" (Psalm 51:3). We must say with the prodigal son, "Father, I have sinned against heaven" (Luke 15:21). When you cry out from a pricked heart and conscience, "God, have mercy on me, a sinner" (Luke 18:13), you are on the way to true repentance. But only on the way; full repentance involves more.

2. Sorrow for Sin

Another aspect of repentance is sorrow for sin. "Godly sorrow brings repentance that leads to salvation" (2 Corinthians 7:10a). This is not mere remorse—not just a feeling of regret and self-pity. Paul calls this latter type "worldly sorrow," and notes that it "brings death" (vs. 10b).

Judas deeply regretted that he had betrayed Jesus. He felt perfectly miserable about what he had done. But he went out and hanged himself. Even though he was seized with remorse at the realization that he had "betrayed innocent blood" (Matthew 27:4), all his sorrow centered in himself. He didn't truly repent, or he would immediately have sought the Savior's forgiveness. His was simply the remorse of any ordinary person who suddenly realizes the horror of what he has done. He's sorry, yes: he's sorry that he was caught, and sorry for the consequences. But that's all.

True sorrow is God-centered. It is a sorrow born of love. One who truly grieves over his sin realizes that he has sinned against God and grieved him. Take an example too often found in our homes. A girl goes out on a date. Her mother tells her to be home before midnight. She doesn't get home until two o'clock. Mother greets her looking both anxious and annoyed. "Jennifer, I couldn't go to bed until you came home. I've really been worried about you. I thought something terrible must have happened to you since you were so late. I'm hurt that you disobeyed me. Why did you do it?" Because Jennifer loves her mother, she begins to realize how thoughtless, selfish and disobedient she has been. "Mother, I'm really sorry that I disobeyed you. I just didn't think about how worried you'd be." And she means it. That is true sorrow. Sorrow for sin must be born out of a love for God. The repentant sinner grieves because he has grieved the one who loves him so.

3. Turning from Sin to Righteousness

But true repentance requires more than admitting our sin and being sorry that it grieves God. The most important thing is to forsake it. One of the words used in Scripture for repentance means "to turn from." Repenting of sin is to turn from sin toward God with a desire to obey him. Repentance means being sorry enough to quit. We will hate and forsake sin because it displeases God. We won't go on trying to enjoy our pet sins. Only a clean and complete break with sin will do (Luke 18:18–22; 2 Corinthians 7:11). The whole direction of our lives will be reversed. There will be a complete about-face. When Saul was converted on the road to Damascus, his very first words were: "What shall I do, Lord?" (Acts 22:10). From then on it was not "What do I, Saul, want?" but "What does the Lord want?" Our daily prayer will be, "Not my will but yours be done."

4. The Fruit of Repentance

When we truly repent, we have a complete change of heart. We now hate the sin that God hates and love what he loves. A result of that change in heart is "fruit in keeping with repentance" (Luke 3:8). Our life begins to show the change in our heart. From that change comes the effort to obey the God to whom we have turned.

But this obedience that springs from repentance doesn't merit God's mercy. As important as repentance is for salvation, all the tears in the world can't make us right with God. God's forgiveness isn't the reward for our tears and fruit of repentance. The purpose of repentance is not to melt the heart of God toward us. The purpose of repentance is to make us conscious of the hopelessness and help-lessness of our sinful condition and lead us, even drive us, to Christ for forgiveness. The more we repent, the more we realize that we repent so imperfectly. Because our repentance is never perfect, we need a Savior.

Faith

The chief requirement for receiving the blessings of Christ's death and resurrection is faith in Jesus Christ. The most important ques-tion in life is "What must I do to be saved?" The answer is from God's Word: "Believe in the Lord Jesus, and you will be saved" (Acts 16:31). Christ taught, "For Gd so loved the world that he gave his one and only Son, that whoever believes in him shall not perish but have eternal life" (John 3:16). Paul wrote, "If you confess with your mouth, 'Jesus is Lord,' and believe in your heart that God raised him from the dead, you will be saved" (Romans 10:9).

Faith is thus the instrument for getting hold of the blessings of Christ's salvation. Therefore we need to know exactly what Chris-tian faith is. What do we mean by faith in Jesus Christ?

1. Based upon Knowledge

Faith in Christ requires a knowledge of Christ. Faith must always have an object, either a person or a thing. No one can have faith in a blank—in nothing. The very nature of faith is to have an object. Christian faith has Christ as the object. Knowing something about Christ is necessary before anyone can believe in Christ.

Fortunately, we don't have to know everything; in fact, the amount that we have to know is very little. God has made the way to Christ so simple that a little child can know it. But however little our knowledge, we must know something. The minimum is found in the words of Paul, "Christ Jesus came into the world to save sin-ners—of whom I am the worst" (1 Timothy 1:15).

This involves knowing who Christ is: the second person of the Trinity, God of very God, the everlasting Son of the Father. This involves knowing certain facts about him: he came into the world, was born of a virgin, lived without sin, and at last was crucified outside Jerusalem. The third day he rose again from the dead. This involves knowing why he died and rose again: he came to save sinners. This involves knowing which sinners he came to save: I am a sinner, the worst of sinners; it was for me he died.

2. A Conviction

Knowing about Christ, however, isn't necessarily the same thing as believing in Christ. Many people know a great deal about Christ. They may have read the Bible from cover to cover many times—but they don't believe in Christ. To have faith in Christ is to be convinced that Christ is the truth. An assent of the mind is necessary. "Yes," says the real believer, "Christ is what he claimed to be, the Son of God."

Faith is a conviction based on evidence sufficient to convince the mind. Unless the intellect is convinced, no one can truly believe. But don't let doubt lead to despair. Christ is very patient and understanding with honest doubters. Even Thomas, one of his own disciples, doubted that Jesus had risen from the dead. He said he would not believe that Christ had risen until he had placed his hand in Christ's side and put his fingers in the nail prints. Listen to Jesus as he talks to this doubting disciple: "Put your finger here; see my hands. Reach out your hand and put it into my side. Stop doubting and believe" (John 20:27).

He extends the same invitation to you. Christ, of all men, welcomes investigation. He knows that the more people honestly investigate him, the more hope exists that they will believe in him. When Thomas saw with his own eyes the risen Christ standing physically before him, he exclaimed, "My Lord and my God!" (John 20:28). Thomas was convinced; the doubter became a believer. Faith is not something apart from, or contrary to, the mind, as some intellectuals would argue. Faith begins with knowledge of the truth, and that knowledge must lead us to a conviction that Jesus is indeed the Son of God.

3. Trust

To stop here would be to miss an essential part of faith. You may *know* a great deal about Christ. You may be *convinced* beyond all doubt that Christ is the Son of the living God. But at best you have only an intellectual faith, what is called a historical faith. You don't yet have saving faith. Faith in Christ that really lays hold of Christ's salvation requires a *trust* in Christ. Scripture says that even the demons believe—and shudder (James 2:19). They know perfectly well who Christ is; they are absolutely convinced of his wisdom, his power and his glory. But they don't trust Christ; they trust themselves. Many people are just like that. They know who Christ is and may even believe that he rose from the dead. But trust him—never! They prefer to trust themselves, their own character or good works. They refuse to trust in the person and work of Christ for salvation.

A poor but discerning Christian woman was once asked what faith was. She answered: "I am ignorant and can't answer very well, but I think it is taking God at his word." How rich in wisdom she was! That is precisely what faith is. It is taking Christ at his word, believing that every promise he makes to us, he is both willing and able to keep.

"Faith in Jesus Christ is a saving grace, whereby we receive and rest upon him alone for salvation, as he is offered to us in the gospel" (SC, Q/A 86). Faith isn't doing something; it isn't earning something. Faith is doing nothing; it is receiving everything. Christ already accomplished the salvation of his people on the cross. The forgiveness of sins and eternal life are gifts to be received. "To all who received him, to those who believed in his name, he gave the right to become children of God" (John 1:12). "I have not merited you by my love, O Christ," said John Calvin. "You have loved me of your free will. I come to you naked and empty, and I find everything here."

A Roman army officer sent messengers to ask Jesus to heal a dying slave. "Lord, don't trouble yourself, for I do not deserve to have you come under my roof. That is why I did not even consider myself worthy to come to you. But say the word, and my servant will be healed" (Luke 7:6, 7). The Roman officer knew about Christ, was convinced of his need for him, and was willing to take him at his word. Jesus was astonished. "I tell you, I have not found such great faith even in Israel" (vs. 9).

That is Christian faith. It takes God at his word, relies on each promise, leans on him in life's trials and trusts him for pardoning grace. And, after receiving Christ, we still must continue to rest in him. Faith is not something we exercise just once in our lives. It is a daily exercise. We live by faith. We are to rest each day in Christ.

4. The Evidence of Saving Faith

"For it is by grace you have been saved, through faith—and this not from yourselves, it is the gift of God—not by works, so that no one can boast. For we are God's workmanship, created in Christ Jesus to do good works, which God prepared in advanced for us to do" (Ephesians 2:8–10). Salvation isn't based on how we live but only on Christ's work on the cross. We receive that work as a gift through faith. Good works don't save, but they are always the result of faith because faith unites us to Jesus Christ. Because of his life *in* us, we *will* do good works. Because we are saved, we will live by faith. Our faith will be "expressing itself through love" (Galatians 2:16, 20; 5:6).

This Christian life that results from true repentance and faith will be the subject of our next chapter.

Review Questions

1. Who came preaching the message of repentance?

2. What are the three elements of true repentance?

3. What kind of sorrow for sin will be evidenced in true repentance?

4. What is the most important element of true repentance?

5. What will be the fruit of true repentance?

6. Is our repentance enough to save us? Why or why not?

7. What must we do to be saved? Answer with a verse of Scripture.

8. What does the knowing the facts about Christ have to do with faith in him?

9. What is the minimum we need to know about Christ in order to be Christians?

10. Can we believe in Christ if we are not convinced that what he has said and done are true?

11. What does Christ invite us to do if we have any honest doubts about him? (John 20:26–31)

12. What is the most important element of faith in Jesus Christ? How was this seen in the Roman officer?

13. What is faith in Jesus Christ? Answer with the Catechism's answer.

14. What is promised to those who believe in Christ?

15. If we are saved by faith, why do good works?

MEMORY WORK
Psalm 1:1–3

Blessed is the man who does not walk in the counsel of the wicked or stand in the way of sinners or sit in the seat of mockers. But his delight is in the law of the Lord, and on his law he meditates day and night. He is like a tree planted by streams of water, which yields its fruit in season and whose leaf does not wither. Whatever he does prospers. (NIV)

Blessed is the man who walks not in the counsel of the ungodly, nor stands in the path of sinners, nor sits in the seat of the scornful; but his delight is in the law of the Lord, and in His law he meditates day and night. He shall be like a tree planted by the rivers of water, that brings forth its fruit in its season, whose leaf also shall not wither; and whatever he does shall prosper. (NKJV)

Questions for Discussion

1. How much faith is necessary for salvation? (Mark 9:20–24)

2. Is everyone who says, "I believe in God," saved? (James 2:19)

3. Do you think we need to be born again by the Holy Spirit before we can believe in Christ? (John 1:12, 13)

4. If not everyone is a child of God, why do *you* repent and believe, and others don't? (Acts 11:18; Acts 13:48)

5. How can we know whether or not we have faith in Christ? (1 John 2:3)

6. Can we lose the assurance of our faith in Christ? How can it be restored?

7. If salvation is by grace through faith alone, how do we explain James 2:24?

8. Do you think we can lose our Christian faith once we truly have it? (Philippians 1:6)

9. Can you have Christian love without Christian faith? (Galatians 5:6)

4

THE CHRISTIAN LIFE

Living Our Confession

As important as Christian faith is, it is not an end in itself. Faith is a means for living life to the glory of God. Faith is for the purpose of life; truth is for the purpose of godliness; salvation is for the purpose of serving God for his glory.

The Purpose of the Christian Life

The purpose of the Christian life is to glorify and enjoy God. "So whether you eat or drink or whatever you do, do it all for the glory of God" (1 Corinthians 10:31). "For from him and through him and to him are all things. To him be the glory forever!" (Romans 11:36). The Christian life is God-centered. A self-centered Christian is a contradiction in terms. A Christian by nature finds God the polestar of his life. As the needle of the compass feels the magnetic pull of the north pole, the Christian turns to God for direction in all his thoughts, affections and purposes.

The first step in Christian living is to dethrone self and bow to Christ as the Lord and King of our lives. Christ said, "If anyone would come after me, he must deny himself and take up his cross and follow me" (Matthew 16:24). When Christ becomes our Savior, he also becomes our Lord. Through his sufferings and death he bought us for himself. From that time on "you are not your own; you were bought at a price. Therefore honor God with your body" (1 Corinthians 6:19, 20).

The same love that saves us also motivates us to live for him who died for us. "For Christ's love compels us, because we are convinced that one died for all, and therefore all died. And he died for all, that those who live should no longer live for themselves but for him who died for them and was raised again" (2 Corinthians 5:14, 15). Christ crucified is not only our salvation; Christ crucified is our example. "To this you were called, because Christ suffered for you, leaving you an example, that you should follow in his steps" (1 Peter 2:21). The Lord himself exhorts us to "be faithful, even to the point of death" (Revelation 2:10). We're all concerned to preserve our own good name. How we live brings either honor or shame to that name. Christians bear the name of Christ. The supreme all-controlling purpose of the Christian life should be to bring honor to the Lord who died for us and whose name we bear.

But what does it mean to "glorify God"? Does it mean simply praising God? This is certainly one way of glorifying him. But far more is involved in glorifying God than singing God's praises, important as that is. To glorify God means essentially to display God's glory in our lives, to reveal God's glory to others. Others should see the glory of God's character in us.

God created all things to reveal his glory. "The heavens declare the glory of God" (Psalm 19:1). "For since the creation of the world God's invisible qualities—his eternal power and divine nature—have been clearly seen, being understood from what has been made" (Romans 1:20). If all creation glorifies God, how much more should *we* glorify him!

God created the human race as the crowning glory of all his creation. He created us in his own likeness. Mankind alone, of all God's creatures, was given a soul. With his soul, man could think about God, trust and love him. "God created man male and female, after his own image, in knowledge, righteousness, and holiness, with dominion over the creatures" (SC, Q/A 10). Man originally reflected the likeness of God in holiness and love.

But then came the tragedy of sin and the fall. The image of God in man became a charred relic of its former self, defaced almost beyond recognition. No longer does the likeness of God exist in man as formerly; the human soul is now dead in transgressions and sins (Ephesians 2:1). Unrighteousness and unholiness predominate. The capacity for knowledge is now used to express hostility toward God.

But this was not the end. The Father sent the Son to be our Savior. Through the redeeming work of Christ, we are not only forgiven and declared righteous before God; we are also restored more and more into mankind's created likeness. When by faith we are vitally connected to Christ, who is the very image of God, we begin to reflect the glory of God's likeness in our lives. "Therefore, if anyone is *in Christ,* he is a new creation; the old has gone, the new has come!" (2 Corinthians 5:17, emphasis added). Paul reminded his readers, "You have…put on the new self, which is being renewed in knowledge in the image of its Creator" (Colossians 3:9, 10). But he exhorted them to continue to "put on the new self, created to be like God in true righteousness and holiness" (Ephesians 4:24). Our constant desire and ambition should be to exhibit more and more the likeness of God, to reflect the divine glory.

The Christian life is a joy as well as a duty. Our aim is to seek to enjoy God. That was why he made us. He made us for himself, to have fellowship with him. Life is empty and cheerless without God's favor and companionship. "You have made us for yourself, and we are restless until we rest in you," said Augustine. Just as God made us for each other socially, he made us for himself spiritually. There is a vacuum in our lives without God's friendship. David confessed, "You will show me the path of life; in your presence is fullness of joy; at your right hand are pleasures forevermore" (Psalm 16:11—NKJV). Jesus taught, "Now this is eternal life: that they may know you, the only true God, and Jesus Christ, whom you have sent" (John 17:3). John wrote: "We proclaim to you what we have seen and heard, so that you also may have fellowship with us. And our fellowship is with the Father and with his Son, Jesus Christ" (1 John 1:3).

All the pleasures of the world leave an aching void. The joys of the Lord satisfy and cause us to sing with the psalmist: "Whom have I in heaven but you? And earth has nothing I desire besides you" (Psalm 73:25). Sin is the one thing that constantly threatens to rob us of this joy. By confessing our sins and turning from them daily, we come to enjoy God's presence more and more. Here is where the purpose to glorify God and the purpose to enjoy God become one. Both are realized only as we strive against sin and do what pleases God. This brings us to the next step in the Christian life.

The Standard for the Christian Life

How can we know what kind of life glorifies God? The same Bible that tells us what to believe tells us also how to live. "The Word of God, which is contained in the Scriptures of the Old and New Testaments, is the only rule to direct us how we may glorify and enjoy him" (SC, Q/A 2).

The Lord Jesus Christ is our example of obedience to God's Word. He perfectly loved the Father and perfectly obeyed his Father's commands. If we love our Lord, we too will keep his commandments. One particular part of the Bible sums up our Lord's standard for the Christian life. It is the Ten Commandments, recorded in Exodus 20:1–17. With your Bible opened to this passage, you will see what is forbidden and what is required in these commandments.

Introduction
(Exodus 20:1, 2) Notice that the Lord doesn't say that if the people keep these commandments, he will save them from bondage. Instead he declares that he has already saved them. Therefore this is how his redeemed people are now to live. The thought of these introductory verses parallels Ephesians 2:8–10. Good works cannot save, but those who are saved must and will do good works in obedience to God's commands. We are saved to serve God and others.

Commandment 1
(Exodus 20:3)—*Whom to Worship. This* commandment teaches that there is only one living and true God, the triune God of the Bible. We are forbidden to worship any god but him. Anything that we value more than God is for all practical purposes our god. Anyone or anything that we love more than God is really our god. What do we think about more than anything else? What do we like to talk about more than anything else? What do we desire above all else? What do we worry about? What do we live for? money? pleasure? perhaps our job or our home? or just ourselves? If so, we are not truly worshiping God alone. God demands first place in our thoughts, in our love, and in all that we do. He wants all of us, not just part of us. He wants us to say from our hearts, "For to me, to live is Christ" (Philippians 1:21).

Commandment 2

(Exodus 20:4–6)—*How to Worship.* This commandment tells us how we are to worship God. We are to worship God using only those specific aspects of worship commanded in his Word. We are not to worship God through things made by men's hands, including images, crucifixes, altars or any other ways not prescribed in Scripture. This commandment also forbids unscriptural imaginings and concepts of God. Any likeness of God made with either our hands or with our minds will be a false and insulting representation. History teaches that the next step is to attach reverence to this likeness and to start worshiping the image in the place of God. "God is spirit," Christ explained, "and his worshipers must worship in spirit and in truth" (John 4:24).

The Lord seeks worship from a heart renewed by the Holy Spirit. He wants us to worship him through the one and only Mediator who is the Truth himself, Jesus Christ. We must avoid other mediators. Beware of an emphasis upon altar, ritual and outward form. These eventually become substitutes for the true worship of the heart. Knowing God and offering him acceptable worship through his Son must be in keeping with Biblical principles.

Commandment 3

(Exodus 20:7)—*Reverence.* God reveals himself through his name. God's names describe his character. We pervert God's intention for his name when we use it in blasphemy, cursing and swearing. God forbids using his name lightly. "You shall not lift up to emptiness" is the literal translation of this commandment. Using God's names, titles or attributes lightly is profaning his name.

Perhaps the most irreverent treatment of God's name is simply to ignore it. To fail to use his name as he intended is also to profane it. Through his name God intended us to learn of him. God's name is revealed in the Bible. To reject any part of God's Word, or neglect to read and obey God's Word, is to profane his name. To think about other things when God's Word is being read or proclaimed in public is to profane his name. "I will worship toward your holy temple, and praise your name for your lovingkindness and your truth; for you have magnified your word above all your name" (Psalm 138:2—NKJV).

The positive intent of this command requires us to use God's name rightly. We are to lift up the name of God and his Son for honor. God wants others to know his name. His name is to be found upon our lips, to tell others of his wisdom, power, holiness, grace and truth. We are to call upon his name in prayer from hearts that love and trust him.

Commandment 4

(Exodus 20:8–11)—*Rest*. This commandment is probably the most widely disobeyed by Christians today. Some teach that Christ and the apostles abolished this commandment. They base this almost entirely on Paul's command, "Therefore do not let anyone judge you by what you eat or drink, or with regard to a religious festival, a New Moon celebration or a Sabbath day. These are a shadow of the things that were to come; the reality, however, is found in Christ" (Colossians 2:16, 17).

To be sure, the food and drink offerings, the sacrifices and ceremonial aspects of the Old Testament Sabbath pointed forward to Christ's work on the cross. These are now done away with. That is why Christ and the apostles substituted the first day of the week in place of the seventh as the Lord's Day. But the moral principle that one day in seven is to be given completely to the Lord was never abrogated by Christ or the apostles. They regarded the Ten Commandments as an unbreakable unit, written by the finger of God. No one commandment was written with erasable ink. Our Lord called upon the leaders of his day to keep all of them (see Luke 10:25–28 and 18:18–22). Christ summed up the whole law and called everyone to keep it (see Matthew 22:37–40).

The principle that one day in seven is set apart for the Lord existed long before the Ten Commandments. In the very beginning, "God blessed the seventh day and made it holy" (Genesis 2:3). God worked six days and rested the seventh and he was refreshed. Being in God's image requires us to pattern our life after his. When we rest from our labors one day in seven, as he did, we too will be refreshed (Exodus 20:11; 31:17; 23:12). The Sabbath was made for humanity as originally created (Mark 2:27, 28). Because mankind is a creature in the likeness of God, he is to pattern his life after God's example of work and rest during the first week of creation.

Jesus upheld the importance of this command by keeping it perfectly. God ordered the day for the sacred assembly of his people (Leviticus 23:3). Our Lord's pattern was to assemble with others in the synagogue and meet separately with his disciples. God set apart the day as a remembrance of the people's deliverance from bondage. The Lord Jesus remembered this deliverance by relieving the bondage of others (Deuteronomy 5:15; Luke 13:16).

By the time of John's exile on the island of Patmos, the first day of the week was already firmly established as the Christian Sabbath. John could testify, "On the Lord's Day I was in the Spirit" (Revelation 1:10). The Old Testament and the New Testament thus agree. A day is still set apart for the Lord. The language here is emphatic. Just as there is a Lord's Supper, a supper set apart to the Lord that we might remember him, so there is still a Lord's Day, a day set apart for him that we might worship and remember him.

It is the Lord's *day*—not hour or morning. The whole day is for physical rest, worship and Christian service. It is a day for receiving from God and service to God. All the worship services of the church should be attended faithfully. (When God's people gather together, we should be there!) Our children are to be taught the things of God's Word in the home. We are to go about helping others: visiting the sick, the lonely, those who need our Christian love. Keep faithfully this one commandment and the growth of your spiritual maturity and your usefulness in Christ's service is assured. Failure to keep this commandment will mean stunted spiritual growth.

Commandment 5

(Exodus 20:12)—*The Home.* This commandment delegates to Christian parents the authority and the duty to govern their children. Through parental training, children should come to know Jesus Christ and discover God's will for their lives. As sinners who are naturally foolish, they will have to be taught (Ephesians 6:4).

Parents must read the Bible with their children regularly. We must tell them what is right and see that they do it. We must encourage them when they do right and correct them when they do wrong (Proverbs 23:13–16). This means that we parents have to know God's Word and model its truths before our children. It means loving, consistent and persistent discipline. Discipline is essential to child training. Children must be taught to listen to, and learn from, their parents, to obey them and to love them. This is the way of blessing for the home, the nation and the church.

Commandment 6

(Exodus 20:13)—*Life.* This commandment has both a positive and a negative side. Negatively, it forbids more than taking one's own or another's life. It forbids anything that injures our own or another's physical well-being. Lack of moderation, overindulgence—even in good things—are killers. Anger and hatred kill. Christ said that we can murder with our words and hearts, as well as with our hands. "Anyone who is angry with his brother," he said, "will be subject to judgment" (Matthew 5:22). Be peacemakers who seek to resolve conflicts God's way and who love your enemies (Matthew 5:23, 24, 44). "Anyone who hates his brother," John wrote, "is a murderer" (1 John 3 :15).

On the positive side, this commandment requires us to do all in our power to preserve our own life and the life of others. Careless disregard of necessary precautions, whether in the home or on the highway, brings death to many each year. Take care of your health and the health of others; get adequate rest to prevent physical and emotional breakdown. Get rid of the sinful habits that harm you physically. Love God by caring for his precious gift of life that he has given to you and to others, including the unborn babies. Love your neighbor as much as you love yourself.

Commandment 7

(Exodus 20:14)—*Purity.* Marriage is a divine institution designed by God to enrich human life and multiply children (Genesis 1:28; 2:18). God has ordained one husband and one wife as the basic unit of society. The marriage bond is intended to be for life. "What God has joined together," our Lord taught, "let man not separate" (Matthew 19:6). Satisfaction of sexual desire within marriage is a gift from the Creator (Proverbs 5:15–21). To satisfy sexual desire outside marriage is forbidden.

But the commandment forbids not just the physical acts of fornication, adultery and homosexuality; even our desires and affections must be pure. "Anyone who looks at a woman lustfully," Christ said, "has already committed adultery with her in his heart" (Matthew 5:28). "Husbands, love your wives, just as Christ loved the church and gave himself up for her." "Wives, submit to your husbands, as to the Lord" (Ephesians 5:25, 22). These are the divine laws for marriage.

Commandment 8

(Exodus 20:15)—*Property*. God as the owner of all things has given to mankind the right to own property. "The heaven, even the heavens, are the Lord's; but the earth he has given to the children of men" (Psalm 115:16—NKJV). As the ultimate owner of all, God has entrusted us as stewards with his created resources. Therefore we must gain and use material possessions according to his rules.

God forbids us to gain wealth through injuring others or to seek to get something for nothing, whether through deceit, unfair wages, deficient work or some form of gambling. We are to work diligently and conserve our income through thrift and economy. We are to do all in our power to promote our neighbor's as well as our own material prosperity. This includes sharing with the poor, especially those who are fellow Christians. "If anyone has material possessions and sees his brother in need but has no pity on him, how can the love of God be in him? Dear children, let us not love with words or tongue but with actions and in truth" (1 John 3:17, 18; see Ephesians 4:28). We are not to rob God by withholding tithes (one-tenth) and offerings. (See Malachi 3:8; Matthew 23:23.)

Commandment 9

(Exodus 20:16)—*The Tongue*. God is a God of truth. He requires his children always to speak the truth. Satan is essentially a deceiver. The word *Devil* means slanderer. "He is a liar and the father of lies" (John 8:44). Lying is the chief way Satan advances his kingdom of error against God's kingdom of truth. He lied in the garden of Eden; he lies today.

Through lying he aims to condemn the godly and to condone the ungodly. Christians must therefore hate all lies, in whatever form they appear. False witnessing in court, malicious slander, and careless gossip all injure the good name of others. This is just what Satan wants. On the contrary, we should be alert to guard our neighbor's character from defamation.

At the same time we must confront our neighbor when he does wrong so that the God of truth may be glorified. We are to follow the example of our Savior who spoke the truth in love to both hypocritical enemies and to stumbling Peter. If our neighbor justly acquires a bad name, we should go directly to him and help him recover a good name rather than tell everyone how bad he is. If he is a Christian, we are to go to him in gentleness and love (Galatians 6:1). If he is not a Christian, we must tell him about the saving grace of God.

Finally, this commandment urges us to speak the truth that Christ is the Savior for our needy world.

Commandment 10

(Exodus 20:17)—*The Heart*. This last commandment concerns the inner desires of the heart. We are not to be discontent, envious or jealous of the reputation or possessions of our neighbor. Instead, rejoice in your neighbor's prosperity. Don't live for material possessions; don't crave them more than anything else. "Watch out!" Christ solemnly warned, "Be on your guard against all kinds of greed; a man's life does not consist in the abundance of his possessions" (Luke 12:15). "What good is it for a man to gain the whole world, yet forfeit his soul?" (Mark 8:36).

Covet most of all the riches of God's grace. "But seek first his kingdom and his righteousness, and all these things will be given to you as well" (Matthew 6:33). Loving God first and most of all, and receiving from him all that his wisdom and goodness entrusts to you, be content with that. Say with Paul, "I know what it is to be in need, and I know what it is to have plenty. I have learned the secret of being content in any and every situation, whether well fed or hungry, whether living in plenty or in want" (Philippians 4:12).

Christ summarized these commandments in one basic law: the law of love. This law is in two parts. "'Love the Lord your God with all your heart and with all your soul and with all your mind. This is the first and greatest commandment. And the second is like it: Love your neighbor as yourself" (Matthew 22:37–39).

The essence of the Christian life is to respond to the gift of God's saving love in Christ, then give ourselves entirely to him; to say with John Calvin, "My heart, O Lord, I give to thee, promptly and sincerely." To love him is to want to keep his commandments. To love him is to love his children, whether his children by creation or by redemption. In fact, if we truly love God, we can't help but love his children. The Ten Commandments show us how to express our love for the Lord and our neighbor in the way that pleases him.

Strength for the Christian Life

How can we live a life of passionate love for God and for people? Certainly not in our own strength. Failure is never so sure in the Christian life as when we think that in our own strength alone we can succeed. "Apart from me," Christ warned, "you can do nothing" (John 15:5). But "I can do everything," Paul said, "through him who gives me strength" (Philippians 4:13). United to Jesus Christ, we have new grace both to *want* and to be *able* to do what pleases him (Philippians 2:13).

The chief resource for spiritual nourishment and growth in grace is God's Word. To grow in grace, therefore, it is essential to be faithful in reading and studying God's Word and in attending public worship.

"Faith comes from hearing the message, and the message is heard through the word of Christ" (Romans 10:17). "Sanctify them by the truth; your word is truth" (John 17:17). "And we, who with unveiled faces all reflect the Lord's glory, are being transformed into his likeness with ever-increasing glory, which comes from the Lord, who is the Spirit" (2 Corinthians 3:18).

In addition to the Word, God has also provided the sacraments and prayer as means to grow in grace. These are the subjects of a later chapter.

Review Questions (Part 1)

1. What is the purpose of the Christian life?

2. What does it mean to "glorify God"?

3. What is it that keeps us from enjoying God?

4. What is the standard for human life?

5. Where do we find the Ten Commandments in the Bible?

6. What do the verses that introduce the Ten Commandments teach us?

7. What other idols besides wood and stone idols do men worship today? (Matthew 6:19–21, 25)

8. How are we to worship God?

9. What is to be our state of mind when God's Word is being read or taught? (1 Peter 1:24–2:3)

10. Are we to keep just part of God's day holy? How are we to keep God's day holy?

MEMORY WORK
1 John 5:2, 3

This is how we know that we love the children of God: by loving God and carrying out his commands. This is love for God: to obey his commands. And his commands are not burdensome. (NIV)

By this we know that we love the children of God, when we love God and keep His commandments. For this is the love of God, that we keep His commandments. And His commandments are not burdensome. (NKJV)

Questions for Discussion (Part 1)

1. What role does Christ have in restoring us to a life that pleases God? (2 Corinthians 5:17; Romans 6:5–11)

2. Why do Christians observe the first day instead of the seventh day of the week as the Christian Sabbath? (Acts 20:7; 1 Corinthians 16:1; Revelation 1:10; John 20:1, 8, 9, 19, 26)

3. What is meant by the teaching "we are not under law, but under grace"? (Romans 6:15) See the context in Romans 6:12–19 and Galatians 3:13.

Review Questions (Part 2)

1. What does the fifth commandment require of parents?

2. What are some forms of murder that are not commonly regarded as murder?

3. What sin of the heart is condemned by the command not to commit adultery?

4. How can we improve our own or our neighbor's material well-being?

5. Why is it important always to tell the truth?

6. What are we to covet most of all? (Matthew 6:33)

7. How did Jesus sum up the moral law?

8. Where do we get the strength to live the Christian life?

Questions for Discussion (Part 2)

1. What principles does the Bible establish for the Christian's giving? (Malachi 3:10; 2 Corinthians 8:2; 1 Timothy 6:6–10, 17–19)

2. What are some rules and regulations that churches sometimes add to the moral law as standards of right and wrong? How scriptural do you think they are? (Mark 7:1)

3. Does the Bible command us to love ourselves first? (2 Timothy 3:2, 4; Philippians 2:4–7, 21; John 12:25 with Mark 8:34, 35)

4. Can a person who is not a Christian live a truly good life? (Compare Luke 6:33 with 1 Corinthians 10:31.)

5

THE CHURCH

Uniting with Others in Our Confession

When you believe in Christ as your personal Savior and Lord, you become a child of the living God. You are adopted into the family of God. Now comes the desire to become a member of a church with others of God's family. You recognize your need for the ministry of the church; you want the fellowship of other Christians; you want to be of some service to your Lord.

But which church should you join? Should you just join the nearest one? Should you look for a big church with a good choir or a church geared to an active social life? Should you choose a small friendly church where they'll call you by your first name? Just what do you look for in a church of Jesus Christ? What is a church? What identifies a true church?

What Is a Church?

The first thing that often comes to mind in thinking of a church is a building, usually with a steeple. Obviously, a church meets in a building, but the building is not the church. A church existed long before any church buildings. The Greek word for "church" in the New Testament was used to identify the Old Testament people of God in the wilderness (Acts 7:38). Several times in his letters Paul speaks of churches meeting in various people's homes. In each case there was no structure that would meet the description of a modern church building.

The church is a body of believers, not a building. Paul speaks of "the church of God, which he bought with his own blood" (Acts 20:28). It is the body of believers for whom Christ died. Paul says of Christ that God "appointed him to be head over everything for the church, which is his body, the fullness of him who fills everything in every way" (Ephesians 1:22, 23). Christ is the head of the church; believers are the body of the church. The body of believers united by faith to Christ, the head, is the church of Christ.

The church is understood in two different senses. There is the *invisible* church, so called because we don't see it. It is the church as God sees it, composed of all those who ever have believed or ever will truly believe in Christ. There are no hypocrites in this church. It is the perfect church, the eternal church. This church will be seen only in heaven.

There is also the *visible* church, the church we see every day all around us. The visible church contains some who profess to believe in Christ but really don't; their hypocrisy may be more or less obvious. In Christ's day the visible church had one member named Judas, who betrayed his Lord. This visible church can be recognized as having a certain external organization, with officers and formal public worship services. The visible church is the topic of this lesson.

A vital relationship exists between Christ and his church. When Peter confessed Christ as the Son of the living God, Christ said, "You are Peter, and on this rock I will build my church, and the gates of Hades will not overcome it" (Matthew 16:18). Here Jesus declares that the apostles (with Peter as their spokesman) are the foundation of his church as they confess and reveal that Jesus is the Christ, the Son of God (Ephesians 2:20; 3:5). "For no one can lay any foundation other than the one already laid, which is Jesus Christ" (1 Corinthians 3:11).

The first thing to examine about any church is its foundation. Is it built on the truth that Jesus is God and Savior? Christ is the only builder of the church. "*I* will build," he says. People can't build a church. Only Christ through his Word and Holy Spirit can create a body of believers.

Christ is also the owner of the church. He calls it "my church." It doesn't belong to any hierarchy, priest or pastor, to any individual or group. Christ alone died for the church. He purchased it with his own blood. It belongs exclusively to him. He alone, therefore, has the right to rule the church. Through his Word we come to know Christ's will for the church. This church, founded upon and built by Christ, is indestructible. Death itself cannot destroy it. Of his kingdom or church there is no end (Matthew 16:18, 19).

In his letter to Timothy, Paul describes some of the basic characteristics of the church. He is concerned for correct behavior "in God's household, which is the church of the living God, the pillar and foundation of the truth" (1 Timothy 3 :15). Timothy was laboring within the shadow of the magnificent temple of Diana of the Ephesians. He might have been tempted to think that the church of Christ suffered in comparison, since Christians held their meetings in a hall or private homes. But what would a person see who looked into the massive temple of Diana? Only a statue of a lifeless goddess.

Do you get the stupendous contrast? Christians may meet in modest surroundings, but they worship in the presence of the God who is alive! God lives in the midst of his church as his household. This teaches us the indescribable privilege of Christian worship. We're not doing God a favor. He is waiting to do a rich favor for us. The living God promises to meet with us heart to heart. As we draw near to him, he intimately draws near to us and lets us know he is with us through his Holy Spirit. We have fellowship with the Father, with the Son, and with one another in Christ.

Incredibly sweet is the fellowship of sinners redeemed by grace, united in faith and love to Christ. Paul reminds Timothy of the high and holy calling of the church; it is "the pillar and foundation of the truth." More magnificent than the stately columns holding up the marble roof of Diana's temple are the living pillars of the church supporting the truth of God's Word. Notice that Paul doesn't say that the church is the truth; no church is perfect. The church is simply the pillar and foundation that supports the truth. As the church faithfully proclaims the truth, sinners receive life and believers grow strong.

Identifying a True Church by its Doctrine and Life

Not every organization that calls itself a church is a true church. Some churches are not committed to the Bible as the Word of God and to Christ as God come in the flesh. Some do not teach biblical repentance and faith. Some churches, Scripture warns, are "synagogues of Satan." How can we identify a true church? Any church worthy of the name Christian must be faithful to the Lord both in doctrine (teaching) and life, remembering that only true doctrine leads to true godliness of life (1 Timothy 6:3).

1. Doctrine

A church faithful to the doctrine of Christ and the Bible will teach the whole will of God (Acts 20:24–27). A faithful church can be identified by its commitment to preaching the Word, administering the sacraments and exercising church discipline.

a. The Preaching of God's Word
A true church will faithfully preach the Word of God. Jesus said, "If you hold to my teaching, you are really my disciples" (John 8:31). "To the law and to the testimony! If they do not speak according to this word, they have no light of dawn" (Isaiah 8:20). "Anyone who runs ahead and does not continue in the teaching of Christ does not have God; whoever continues in the teaching has both the Father and the Son" (2 John 9).

After visiting a church, ask yourself, "Do I know more about the Bible? Has the minister faithfully worked to explain what God says in his Word? Through his preaching, have I come to see my sin and God's glory more clearly? Were the doctrines of God's grace proclaimed fully? Has my faith been strengthened, my love for Christ and others deepened?" If not, you are in the wrong church and should leave it (Romans 16:17).

b. The Administration of the Sacraments
The proper administration of the sacraments is an essential aspect of a church committed to Christ and true faith in him. The next chapter will deal with the sacraments in more detail. Meanwhile, the Scriptures tell us the true meaning of the sacraments and how they are to be administered. A church that doesn't follow the Bible in the use of the sacraments is not a true church.

Christ and the apostles taught emphatically that salvation is by grace through faith alone, not through the sacraments. To be cut off from the sacraments is not to be cut off from salvation. To teach contrary to this is not the mark of a true church. Paul solemnly warned that only true believers who are living obedient lives may partake of the Lord's Supper. "Examine yourselves to see whether you are in the faith; test yourselves" (2 Corinthians 13:5; 1 Corinthians 11:28). A church, therefore, that permits men who don't believe that Christ is God to administer the sacraments is not a true church. Neither is one that administers the sacraments to those whose lives are openly scandalous.

c. The Exercise of Church Discipline

A true church will accompany the preaching of the Word and the administration of the sacraments with the consistent exercise of church discipline. Christ distinctly instructed the church to discipline its members. If anyone continues in his sins, "tell it to the church; and if he refuses to listen even to the church, treat him as you would a pagan or a tax collector" (Matthew 18:15–20). Paul wrote to the church at Corinth demanding them to put an unrepentant, sexually immoral person out of the assembly (1 Corinthians 5:1–5).

One purpose of discipline is to restore the disobedient by leading them to repentance. "Brothers, if someone is caught in a sin, you who are spiritual should restore him gently" (Galatians 6:1; James 5:19, 20). The other purpose is to preserve the honor of Christ and the purity of his church. When a person denies Christ or continues in blatant sin, a threefold injury occurs in not exercising church discipline. 1) We injure the sinner who needs to be restored. It's simply unkind not to try to regain him. 2) We hurt the church. The whole church will be infected unless wrong doctrine or immoral behavior is uprooted. 3) We injure the honor of Christ whose name we bear. The church becomes an object of scorn before the world.

A church that doesn't love the body of Christ or the head of the church enough to try to keep Christ's members pure in doctrine and life is not a church to be trusted with the nurture of our souls. At the other extreme, when a church uses discipline to uproot the believer and the righteous—as Rome did with Luther in the 16th century and as the Presbyterian Church in the U.S.A. did with J. Gresham Machen in the early 20th century—it has distorted the purposes of church discipline.

2. Life

A true church will be one whose teaching is affecting its life; the truth of God will be visibly changing people's lives (Romans 12:1, 2). The change will be reflected in the faith, hope, love and holiness of the members.

a. Faith, Hope and Love

The apostle Paul described the Colossian church as characterized by faith, hope and love. "We always thank God, the Father of our Lord Jesus Christ, when we pray for you, because we have heard of your *faith* in Christ Jesus and of the *love* you have for all the saints— the faith and love that spring from the *hope* that is stored up for you in heaven and that you have already heard about in the word of truth, the gospel that has come to you. All over the world this gospel is bearing fruit and growing, just as it has been doing among you since the day you heard it and understood God's grace in all its truth" (Colossians 1:3–6, emphasis added).

In a similar way, Paul described the powerful working of God's Word and Spirit in the church in Thessalonica. "We always thank God for all of you, mentioning you in our prayers. We continually remember before our God and Father your work produced by *faith*, your labor prompted by *love*, and your endurance inspired by *hope* in our Lord Jesus Christ. For we know, brothers loved by God, that he has chosen you...." (1 Thessalonians 1:2–4, emphasis added).

In visiting a church, we must ask, "Is there faith? Do the people express confidence and trust in Christ, the head of the church? Is there hope? Do the people show Christian stability and endurance in this life because they confidently expect a future home in heaven? Is there love?" This is the most important mark of all. "And now these three remain: faith, hope and love. But the greatest of these is love" (1 Corinthians 13:13).

While love is certainly the greatest of the permanent gifts, it is accompanied by many misconceptions. True Christian love doesn't mean a toleration of unbelief and sinful living. "Love does not delight in evil but rejoices with the truth" (1 Corinthians 13:6). Real love isn't indifferent to the sin that harms those who practice it, as well as their victims, but makes every effort to bring them to repentance through discipline (Hebrews 12:6, 12–15; Revelation 3:19; Proverbs 13:24). However, the preaching of the Word and church discipline unaccompanied by love become a harsh tyranny that drives people away from Christ. "If I speak in the tongues of men and of angels, but have not love, I am only a resounding gong or a clanging cymbal" (1 Corinthians 13:1).

Love builds others up in the church by speaking the truth in love and by encouraging others to use their gifts, abilities and possessions for ministry (Ephesians 4:15, 16). Love feels the needs of others and moves us to open our homes in Christian hospitality (Romans 12:10, 13). We exercise true Christian love because our faith and hope are different from the world's. While we wait for Christ's coming, every true body of believers desires to be an instrument of Christ's love to do good to all men, especially to the Christian family (Galatians 6:10; 1 Timothy 6:17–19).

b. Holiness

The church of Christ is called a "holy nation" (1 Peter 2:9, 10). A true church will have members that are growing to be more like their holy Lord. They will reflect a clean break with sin (Romans 6:5–19). They have "put on the new self, created to be like God in true righteousness and holiness" (Ephesians 4:24). They are seeking to become more holy, knowing that "without holiness, no one will see the Lord" (Hebrews 12:14). This doesn't mean that you will find perfect people in a true church, or that a true church is perfect. (If you find a perfect church and join it, it won't be perfect anymore!) But what you must look for is a body of believers who, by God's grace, are aware of their sins and are growing out of them, striving to be more obedient to the Lord.

There are many churches that are seeking to be faithful to the Lord in doctrine and life. How do you decide which of these true churches to join? Each denomination has certain distinctive doctrines that set it apart from others. Examine their teachings fairly, compare them with Scripture, and rely on the Holy Spirit to help you determine which one is closest to the Word of God in its teachings.

We would like to set forth the distinctive teachings of true Presbyterian and Reformed churches so you can examine them in the light of God's Word.

True Presbyterian and Reformed Churches

An alert observer will note different kinds of churches calling themselves "Presbyterian" or "Reformed." The differences aren't in local names such as "First," "Fifth Avenue," "Calvary," or "New Hope." These are simply names that distinguish one local Presbyterian or Reformed church from another. They tell us nothing about the beliefs of that particular church. The differences we want to pinpoint are differences in doctrine and practice among churches that have the same generic name—Presbyterian, or Reformed.

Basically, there are two different kinds of churches that go by the name Presbyterian or Reformed. One group believes the Bible in its entirety to be the Word of God and adheres to the historic creeds of the Presbyterian and Reformed faith, such as the Westminster Confession of Faith, the Belgic Confession and the Canons of Dordt. The other no longer confesses that the Bible in its entirety is God's Word and doesn't accept the historic creeds of the Reformed faith as its confessional basis. Some churches in this second group have adopted a radically different confession; others are extensively modifying their creed and practice. Only churches in the first category are faithfully Presbyterian and Reformed.

Your class instructor will present the origin and doctrinal commitment of your particular church's denomination

Presbyterian Means Being Governed by Elders

What difference does it make how a church is governed as long as it teaches the Bible and preaches the gospel? This is a very common attitude today toward church government. And yet the Bible has something to say about how a church is to be organized and governed. The Christian must always be concerned to know what the Bible teaches about any matter and hold to that teaching.

History shows that it makes a tremendous difference how the church is governed. Some have believed with the Roman Catholic Church that the church should rule the state. Others have believed with the Church of England that the state should rule the church.

Both of these views have brought untold bloodshed and injury to both church and state. John Calvin rediscovered the biblical teaching that both the state and the church are organized and ordained by God. The state is not to govern the church; Christ governs the church through the leaders he chooses. The church is not to rule the state; it is to instruct the state to encourage and protect righteousness (1 Peter 2:14; Proverbs 14:34; Deuteronomy 17:18, 19). The rediscovery of these truths has brought great peace and prosperity to both church and state. The Presbyterian form of government conforms to the principle that the Scriptures are sufficient to define the roles of church and state.

The three chief forms of government employed in churches today are the hierarchical (rule by a sacred order), congregational (rule by the congregation) and presbyterian (rule by presbyters or elders). The Roman Catholic, Episcopalian and Methodist churches have the hierarchical type of government in varying forms and degrees. The Baptist, Independent Fundamental, and Congregational churches have the congregational form of government in varying forms and degrees.

Which of these three forms of government does the Bible teach? Presbyterians believe the Bible teaches that the church is to be ruled by elders (*presbyters* in the Greek). From this word *presbyter*, translated "elder," the Presbyterian church derives its name. It is a church ruled by elders. It means that we believe the Bible is sufficient even to tell us how the church is to be organized and ruled. In speaking of the men who are to lead God's people, we read, "Let the elders [presbyters] who rule well be counted worthy of double honor, especially those who labor in the word and doctrine" (1 Timothy 5:17—NKJV).

The church is thus to be governed by two kinds of elders, *ruling* elders and *teaching* elders. These elders are also called bishops, or overseers (Titus 1:5, 7). They are shepherds set apart to nurture God's people (Acts 20:17, 28; Hebrews 13:7, 17). Deacons are another set of officers who are chosen to minister to needy Christians (Acts 6:1–7).

The apostles and elders of the New Testament church gathered for a general council to determine matters of Christian faith and practice (Acts 15:6ff.). This teaches the need for general assemblies of the whole church such as exists in the Presbyterian system. Local congregations in isolation from each other are not the framework of church government reflected in the practice of the early church. Such independency is unknown in the New Testament.

Reformed in Doctrine

The chief difference between Presbyterian and other churches, however, is not in government but in doctrine. The teaching of the Presbyterian churches is set forth in the Westminster Confession of Faith.

The Westminster Confession was formulated (1643–48) under the direction of the Parliament of England by 121 ordained teachers, 11 lords and 20 commoners. It is the most universally accepted creed of Protestantism. The teachings of this confession are called "The Reformed Faith."

What does this confession teach that is not found in the other creeds of Christendom? It is the teaching of the sovereignty of God. God is held to be absolutely supreme in wisdom, power, holiness, truth and grace. In all his works of creation, providence and redemption, God orders all things for his own glory. God is in control of a sparrow falling to the ground, of the decisions of a king, and of bringing us all our trials (Matthew 10:29; Proverbs 21:1; 1 Thessalonians 3:3). The throne of his kingdom rules over *all* (Psalm 103:19). "For from him and through him and to him are all things. To him be the glory forever!" (Romans 11:36).

This means that salvation, too, is all of God; God controls both the accomplishment of salvation in history and the application of salvation to individual lives today. The supreme control of God over human salvation has been challenged at five crucial points. The Presbyterian and Reformed churches have stated five vital truths in answer to these objections. They are:

1. Total Depravity of Man.

Man is totally sinful in his intellect, affections and will. Man is not just sick with sin; he is dead in sin. Man is "utterly indisposed, disabled and made opposite to all good, and wholly inclined to all evil" (WCF, chap. 6, sec. 4). Scripture confirms this doctrine. "The sinful mind is hostile to God. It does not submit to God's law, nor can it do so. Those controlled by the sinful nature cannot please God" (Romans 8:7, 8). "Every inclination of his heart is evil from childhood" (Genesis 8:21). "There is no one who understands, no one who seeks God" (Romans 3:11). "You were dead in your transgressions and sins" (Ephesians 2:1). "The Lord saw how great man's wickedness on the earth had become, and that every inclination of the thoughts of his heart was only evil all the time" (Genesis 6:5).

2. Unconditional Election.

This is the biblical teaching that God in his love chose from among totally sinful human beings some that he would redeem to himself while passing others by. God's decision wasn't based on anything in these individuals or on anything he foresaw they would become. They were as hostile to him as the rest of mankind, but he simply loved them. Why he didn't love *all* is no mystery. No one deserves his love. Why he loved *any* is the profound mystery. Jesus taught the doctrine of election when he said, "You did not choose me, but I chose you and appointed you that you should go and bear fruit" (John 15:16—NKJV).

Many other Scripture passages provide the basis of this doctrine. Here are just a few. "He *chose* us in him before the creation of the world to be holy and blameless in his sight. In love he *predestined* us to be adopted as sons through Jesus Christ, in accordance with his pleasure and will....In him we were also *chosen*, having been *predestined* according to the plan of him who works out everything in conformity with the purpose of his will" (Ephesians 1:4, 5, 11, emphasis added). "And all who were *appointed* for eternal life believed" (Acts 13:48, emphasis added).

Unconditional election relates to the next truth. Those whom God chose before the foundation of the world are the ones registered in the Lamb's book as those for whom he died (Revelation 13:8; 1 Peter 1:1, 2).

3. Definite Atonement.

When Christ died on the cross for our sins, he died with the intention, not of saving every single person in the whole mass of humanity, but of saving a definite number of people—all those whom the Father had chosen from before the foundation of the world.

Here are some of the numerous passages that support this teaching. "You are to give him the name Jesus, because he will save *his people* from their sins" (Matthew 1:21). "I lay down my life for *the sheep* (John 10:15). "I am not praying for the world, but for *those* you have given me" (John 17:9). "*Those* he predestined, he also called; *those* he called, he also justified" (Romans 8:30; emphasis added in the above quotations).

As the diagram below shows, on the cross Jesus Christ suffered the pains of Hell in the place of his own people.

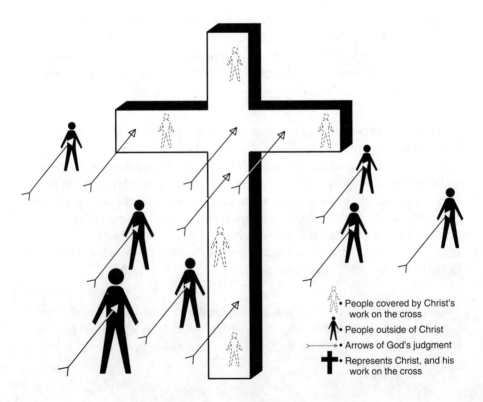

- People covered by Christ's work on the cross
- People outside of Christ
- Arrows of God's judgment
- Represents Christ, and his work on the cross

Christ experienced the arrows of God's wrath upon himself in their stead. None of the arrows of God's judgment will reach Christ's own people. However, if Christ had died to save all, even though it is obvious that all are not saved, then Christ would have failed. God is no longer God. In such a case, Christ could *actually* save no one. He could only make salvation *possible*.

No one can bring a charge against God's elect because Jesus is their substitute. He bore the penalty of eternal death in their place (Romans 8:33–35). Christ has shielded them from the arrows of God's judgment. But he hasn't done so for others. These will receive the arrows of God's eternal wrath.

Jesus didn't die to make salvation a possibility for all, but a reality for his own by dying in their place. The question, "For whom did Christ die?" is answered by understanding the purpose of Christ's death. Christ died to actually *save* his own. The only safety for you is to belong to Christ and be hidden in him from God's judgment (Romans 8:1, 29, 30). In Christ, there is complete safety. Do you belong to Christ?

4. Irresistible Grace.

When the Holy Spirit comes to make someone a new creature in Christ, no one can prevent or resist that work. Jesus promised that "all that the Father gives me will *come* to me" (John 6:37). He said moreover to Nicodemus, "The wind *blows wherever* it pleases....So it is with everyone born of the Spirit" (John 3:8, emphasis added in the above quotations).

If anyone can resist the Spirit of God, he is stronger than God. God is no longer God; man is supreme. The only way a person who is naturally hostile to God and dead in sin will ever come to Christ is through God himself taking the initiative to work in his heart to draw him. All are invited to come to Christ. No one who comes will be turned away. But when you come to Christ, don't pat yourself on the back—rather, praise the sovereign God who brought you to himself (John 6:44, 37).

5. The Preservation and the Perseverance of Believers.

Once we believe, we will be kept by God and persevere in faith to the end. This doesn't mean we may not fall into sin. As Spurgeon put it, we may fall many times on the deck of the ship of life, but we shall never fall overboard (see Psalm 37:24). God doesn't cast off those whom he has loved. He doesn't undo the work of grace he began.

Here are some passages that clearly teach this. "I give them eternal life, and they shall never perish; no one can snatch them out of my hand" (John 10:28). "Being confident of this, that he who began a good work in you will carry it on to completion until the day of Christ Jesus" (Philippians 1:6; 1 Peter 1:5). "I am convinced that neither death nor life, neither angels nor demons, neither the present nor the future, nor any powers, neither height nor depth, nor anything else in all creation, will be able to separate us from the love of God that is in Christ Jesus our Lord" (Romans 8:38, 39). The God who begins our salvation will see it through to the end, in order to receive our praise forever (Romans 11:36).

Review Questions (Part 1)

1. Once we are children in God's family, why will we want to become a member of a church?

2. What is a church?

3. Who is the foundation, builder and owner of the church?

4. Who dwells in the midst of the church?

5. There are so many different churches. How can we recognize a true church of Christ?

6. How will faithfulness to God's truth affect a church's doctrine? its life?

7. What are the purposes of church discipline? (Matthew 18:15–20; 1 Corinthians 5)

8. How will Christian love show itself in the life of a true church?

9. Describe Presbyterian government by elders.

MEMORY WORK
1 Peter 2:9, 10

But you are a chosen people, a royal priesthood, a holy nation, a people belonging to God, that you may declare the praises of him who called you out of darkness into his wonderful light. Once you were not a people, but now you are the people of God; once you had not received mercy, but now you have received mercy. (NIV)

But you are a chosen generation, a royal priesthood, a holy nation, His own special people, that you may proclaim the praises of Him who called you out of darkness into His marvelous light; who once were not a people but are now the people of God, who had not obtained mercy but now have obtained mercy. (NKJV)

Questions for Discussion (Part 1)

1. What might we say to someone who says, "I don't need to be a member of a church. It's okay for you, but not for me."?

2. What are some of the privileges of being a member of a true church?

3. What are some of the responsibilities of being a member of a

true church?

4. What is involved in publicly confessing Christ as "Lord"?

5. Is membership in secret religious organizations that do not confess faith in Christ consistent with membership in a Christian church?

6. What does Christ think of a church that doesn't exercise church discipline? (Revelation 2:14–16, 20; Revelation 2:4–6)

7. What should you do if one of the elders in your church denies that Jesus is God, and the local elders do not listen to your concern?

Review Questions (Part 2)

1. What is the teaching of the Presbyterian and Reformed churches that other churches de-emphasize or neglect?

2. Give a Bible verse describing the extent of human sinfulness.

3. What is meant by unconditional election?

4. For whom did Christ die?

5. If we are naturally hostile to God, how can anyone come to Christ?

6. Can a saved person lose his eternal life? Prove your answer from the Bible.

Questions for Discussion (Part 2)

1. Is God truly in control of all things if he is not in control of saving people?

2. Does the teaching that Christ died just for those whom the Father in love had chosen make God unfair? (Romans 9:16–23)

3. Does the teaching of God's electing love deny that we should freely and sincerely offer the gospel to everyone? (John 6:35–37, 44, 45, 65)

4. Would God still be God if he intended to have Christ save everyone but was frustrated by man?

5. How does the teaching of the perseverance of the saints differ from the teaching that "once you are saved, you are always saved, no matter how you live"? (1 Peter 1:5; 2 Peter 1:1–11)

6

GOD'S PROVISION FOR GROWTH

God Nurtures Those Who Confess Christ

Peter urged those who had been brought to faith in Christ to "grow in the grace and knowledge of our Lord and Savior Jesus Christ" (2 Peter 3:18). Plants grow as they are watered, fertilized and given proper sunlight. Once God makes you his child, he waters and fertilizes your new life to enable you to grow.

God nourishes us with the Word of God, the sacraments and prayer in the soil of Christian fellowship. These are his means to enable us to grow more like Christ and to give a firm confession of faith in him.

The Word of God

Reading God's Word and hearing his Word preached strengthens our faith and sanctifies our souls. Saying goodbye to the Ephesian elders, Paul declared, "Now I commit you to God and to the word of his grace, which can build you up and give you an inheritance among all those who are sanctified" (Acts 20:32). Jesus prayed, "Sanctify them by the truth; your word is truth" (John 17:17). Peter reminds us that the Word we hear preached is God's eternal Word, and therefore, "like newborn babies, long for the pure milk of the word, that by it you may grow in respect to salvation" (1 Peter 2:2—NASB).

But the Word of God doesn't automatically bless those who hear it. Paul described his message as conveying the aroma of death to some and of life to others (2 Corinthians 2:14–17). How then should the Word of God be read and heard in order to produce the blessings of salvation? "That the Word may become effectual to salvation, we must attend thereunto with diligence, preparation, and prayer; receive it with faith and love, lay it up in our hearts, and practice it in our lives" (SC, Q/A 90).

With diligence—Read regularly and carefully; try to understand what you read.

Preparation—Have a plan. You might, for example, alternate between an Old Testament book and a New Testament book. Have helps nearby such as a reliable Bible handbook, a good Bible dictionary or a sound commentary—and use them.

Prayer—Ask the Holy Spirit to cause you not only to understand the passage but to apply it to your life (Psalm 119:18; Luke 11:13).

With faith—Pay attention to the warning of the writer to the Hebrews: "But the message they heard was of no value to them, because those who heard did not combine it with faith" (Hebrews 4:2).

And with love—"Oh, how I love your law! I meditate on it all day long" (Psalm 119:97).

Lay it up in our hearts—Memorize, and meditate upon, God's Word. (Psalm 119:11; Deuteronomy 31:19).

Practice it in our lives—Obey the Word you read and hear preached. "Do not merely listen to the word, and so deceive yourselves. Do what it says" (James 1:22).

The Sacraments

"A Sacrament is a holy ordinance instituted by Christ; wherein, by sensible [i.e., physical] signs, Christ, and the benefits of the new covenant, are represented, sealed, and applied to believers" (SC, Q/A 92). Just as no automatic blessing accompanies the written Word of God, so no automatic blessing accompanies these "visual" words of God. To be nourished and grow as we receive the sacraments, the Holy Spirit must give us faith in the truths the sacraments represent.

Only two sacraments were instituted by Christ: baptism and the Lord's Supper. In accordance with Scripture, every Christian church requires its members to receive these two ordinances. Two extremes can be found in churches today regarding both of these sacraments. The one exalts the sacraments above the preaching of God's Word;

the other belittles them. As always, we must turn to the Scriptures for the real meaning of the sacraments and the proper emphasis they should have.

1. Baptism

Baptism is clearly commanded by Christ. Among his very last instructions to his disciples was the order, "Therefore go and make disciples of all nations, baptizing them in the name of the Father and of the Son and of the Holy Spirit" (Matthew 28:19). The meaning of baptism is what has to be explored.

The water of baptism has no power to save. The forgiveness of sins is accomplished by Christ on the cross and received by faith alone. This faith is made possible through the Word of God alone and not through baptism. "Consequently, faith comes from hearing the message, and the message is heard through the word of Christ" (Romans 10:17; see vss. 9, 10). On the other hand, baptism is more than just a nice little ceremony that has no significance beyond the external act.

a. A Sign of God's Grace

Baptism is an outward sign of an inward grace. It represents what takes place in the soul of one who believes in Jesus Christ.

The first and the most important thing that baptism represents is the believer's union with Christ. Baptism represents and seals to us the fact that we have been united to Christ by faith. The Lord's command to baptize, literally translated, reads, "Baptizing them *in[to]* the name of the Father and of the Son and of the Holy Spirit" (Matthew 28:19, emphasis added). Paul speaks of being "baptized into his death" (Romans 6:3) and "baptized into Christ" (Galatians 3:27). By faith we are truly united to the Father, the Son and the Holy Spirit.

The outward sign used in baptism is water. Water in the Scriptures is most frequently associated with cleansing. The inward grace that water signifies is purification from both the *guilt* and the *pollution* of sin. Baptism pictures the fact that we have been cleansed from the guilt of our sins through the atoning blood of Christ. Ananias declared to Paul, "Get up, be baptized and wash your sins away, calling on his name" (Acts 22:16).

Baptism also represents the fact that we have been cleansed from the pollution or defilement of sin. We enter the kingdom only by being born again by the Spirit of God. Jesus said, "No one can see the kingdom of God unless he is born again" (John 3:3). Our Lord found water an appropriate symbol to represent cleansing from the defilement of sin that takes place in the new birth. He said: "No one can see the kingdom of God unless he is born of water and the Spirit" (John 3:5). Baptism represents our entrance into the kingdom. To enter the kingdom of God we must be cleansed from the guilt of our sins through the redeeming blood of Christ, and cleansed from the pollution of our sins through the operation of the Spirit of God. As the outward representation of this inward cleansing from the guilt and pollution of our sins (Titus 3:5, 6), baptism is given to help you grow up as a Christian. It dispels false assurance as it calls you to ask, "Do I have the inner reality that is represented?" It helps you come to full assurance as you look in faith to Christ and his cleansing. And it also urges you to live for Christ. You have been baptized! Your sins have been washed away! Will you now go on living in your sin? "We were therefore buried with him through baptism into death in order that, just as Christ was raised from the dead through the glory of the Father, we too may live a new life (Romans 6:4; see vss. 1–11).

b. A Seal of God's Promise
Baptism is also a seal; it confirms and establishes to us the blessings pictured. Just as a seal on a diploma confirms the testimony contained in it, so baptism confirms and establishes to us the benefits of God's covenant of grace. Circumcision in the Old Testament was God's external seal of his spiritual covenant promises to Abraham. "And he received the sign of circumcision, a seal of the righteousness that he had by faith" (Romans 4 :11). Baptism in the New Testament, as we will see more clearly below, simply takes the place of circumcision in the Old Testament (Colossians 2:11, 12); therefore baptism is now God's seal of his covenant promises to us. God has promised that we will be his, and he ours, in all the blessings of his saving grace. He has promised that our sins are really washed away when we trust in Christ alone. To confirm and establish these promises of grace, he gives us the seal of baptism.

A fundamental difference exists among Protestants on the question of who should be baptized. Some hold that baptism is for believers only. Most Protestants hold that baptism is not only for believers but for their children as well. What do the Scriptures teach about this?

Clearly, children of believers in the Old Testament received the sign of God's covenant of grace. God's promises were for the believer and his household. All who received the covenant promise, including eight-day-old boys, were to receive circumcision as a sign of God's promise (Genesis 17:7–10). If children of believers are now, in the New Testament period, to be excluded from God's covenant of grace, we would need some clear statement in Scripture that this is the case. We have no such statement. In fact, we have clear teaching that they *are* to be included.

The Lord promised that when the Messiah came, his everlasting covenant would continue to be with believers and their children (Jeremiah 32:38–40; Isaiah 59:20, 21). The fulfillment of this promise came at Pentecost when Peter declared, "The promise is for you *and your children*" (Acts 2:39, emphasis added). When parents who believed brought their infants to Jesus, he took them up in his arms and blessed them, saying, "The kingdom of God belongs to such as these" (Mark 10:14). Paul affirmed that even if only one parent is a believer, the children are declared holy (1 Corinthians 7:14), and set apart for God, just as the covenant children of the Old Testament were (Ezekiel 16:20, 21).

There is only one covenant of grace, only one way of salvation, in both the Old and the New Testaments. "Your father Abraham rejoiced at the thought of seeing my day," said Jesus. "He saw it and was glad" (John 8:56). "Abraham believed God," wrote Paul, "and it was credited to him as righteousness" (Romans 4:3).

The oneness of God's plan of redemption in both the Old and the New Testament periods demands consistency. If children were included in the covenant of grace in the Old Testament period, they must be included in the New Testament period as well. Thus baptism in the New Testament has the same meaning as circumcision in the Old Testament and simply replaces it. "In him you were also circumcised, in the putting off of the sinful nature, not with a circumcision done by the hands of men but with the circumcision done by Christ, having been buried with him in baptism and raised with him through your faith in the power of God, who raised him from the dead" (Colossians 2:11, 12).

If baptism has the same meaning as circumcision—which involved children—how can we exclude children from baptism? Lydia "and the members of her household were baptized" (Acts 16:15); the Philippian jailer "and all his family were baptized" (Acts 16:33); Paul "baptized the household of Stephanas" (1 Corinthians 1:16). While such passages can't prove that children were present in these households, only sheer prejudice would affirm that none were. The principle still stands that every member in the family's household should receive the sign of God's promise.

This doesn't mean, and never has meant, that the children of believers are automatically saved. In the Old Testament, those who received the sign of the covenant were called to repent and experience the inward reality that the sacrament represented. "Circumcise yourselves to the Lord, and remove the foreskins of your heart....Wash your heart from evil, O Jerusalem, that you may be saved" (Jeremiah 4:4, 14—NASB). In the same way, we must call our covenant children to repentance and to trust in the promises represented in their baptism. Only such children as truly trust in the promises of God are in fact children of the promise and enjoy God's salvation (Romans 9:8; Psalm 103:17, 18).

The particular methods of baptism would prove an interesting and profitable study. It is enough to say here that our Lord didn't prescribe how much water was necessary. We may not therefore dogmatically assert that only immersion or only sprinkling is correct.

c. The Believer's Response

God promises grace to the children of believing parents. Believing parents claim that promise. They also recognize God's claim upon their children; they are the Lord's. Therefore, parents present their children to receive the sign and seal of God's covenant of grace.

At baptism, Christian parents respond to questions concerning their children. First, the believing parent claims God's promise to regard the child as His. Second, they promise God to instruct the child in the Christian faith. The questions are worded in the following or a similar way:

1. Do you acknowledge that, although our children are conceived and born in sin and therefore are subject to condemnation, they are holy in Christ, and as members of his church ought to be baptized?

2. Do you promise to instruct your child in the principles of our holy religion as revealed in the Scriptures of the Old and New Testaments, and as summarized in the Confession of Faith and Catechisms of this church; and do you promise to pray with and for your child, to set an example of holiness and godliness before him, and with God's help to use all the means that he has appointed to bring him up in the discipline and instruction of the Lord?

In claiming God's promise of grace, parents are expressing confidence in their child's inheritance and security in Christ. Parents may confidently expect that God will fulfill his promise of grace to their child. Much of the child's spiritual good, however, will depend on the parents' keeping these vows. As with Abraham, your own example and instruction are God's means to bring about the blessing of salvation he has promised your children (Genesis 18:18, 19).

As Christian parents, we must pray intensely that the Holy Spirit will produce in our children the inward cleansing and regeneration represented in their baptism. Pray that your children will, as David, learn to trust in the Lord from their earliest days (Psalm 22:9, 10).

2. The Lord's Supper

When he observed the Passover with his disciples, Christ instituted the sacrament of the Lord's Supper. As baptism was the unbloody replacement of circumcision, so the Lord's Supper was intended as the unbloody replacement for the feast of Passover. Christ was to be the Passover Lamb who would take away our sins and keep away the angel of death. Taking in his hands the elements of bread and wine, our Lord said, "This is my body given for you; do this in remembrance of me....This cup is the new covenant in my blood, which is poured out for you" (Luke 22:19, 20). In our fellowship at the Lord's Supper, the elements that we share remind us that Christ is the common source of life that binds us together. "Is not the cup of thanksgiving for which we give thanks a participation in the blood of Christ? And is not the bread that we break a participation in the body of Christ? Because there is one loaf, we, who are many, are one body, for we all partake of the one loaf" (1 Corinthians 10:16, 17).

The divisions that have arisen over the meaning of this sacrament in the history of the church are regrettable. Roman Catholicism teaches that the bread and the wine become the actual flesh and blood of Christ. The elements lifted in the mass before the altar supposedly undergo a complete change into the actual flesh and blood of Christ. Christ is thus resacrificed again and again for the sins of his people.

Lutheranism teaches that Christ is bodily present in, with and under the elements of bread and wine. This view holds that Christ in his human nature is present on this earth. This is contrary to Scripture, which teaches that Christ in his human nature ascended into heaven, where he will remain until he returns bodily in power and great glory.

Both of these teachings involve pressing too far the interpretation of the words of Jesus, "This *is* my body....This *is* my blood" (Matthew 26:26, 28, emphasis added). The meaning is clear, they say, and allows of no other interpretation than to say the bread and wine are Jesus' actual body and blood. However, the verb "is" doesn't always mean "equivalent to" or "same as." Jesus used the same verb when he said, "I *am* the vine." Certainly he didn't mean to say that he was an actual grapevine. As Jesus stood there in his body holding a piece of bread, he wasn't saying that his body actually was the bread he was holding. Obviously the word "is" means "represents."

a. A Memorial of Christ's Atonement

The Lord's Supper is a memorial: "Do this in remembrance of me." It reminds us specifically of his death. It was not his life, not his miracles, not his teachings, but his death that he wanted us to remember above all else.

The Lord's Supper is a symbol, a representation of Christ's body and blood. The broken bread represents his broken body. The wine that is poured represents his shed blood. He tells us why his body was broken and his blood was shed: "This is my body....This is my blood of the covenant, which is poured out for many for the forgiveness of sins" (Matthew 26:26, 28). This sacrament portrays Christ dying in our place, paying the penalty of our sins.

b. A Sign and Seal of God's Grace

The Lord's Supper is a sign and seal of God's covenant of grace. "This is my blood of the covenant," our Lord declared (Matthew 26:28). He gives us this external emblem of his blood to assure us. He guarantees to fulfill his promises of grace and salvation to everyone who partakes by faith. As you take the cup, look to the work of Christ that it represents. God is speaking to you in a visual way. He is saying that your sins really are washed away by the blood of Christ.

The Lord's Supper is also a fellowship. "Is not the cup of thanksgiving for which we give thanks a participation in the blood of Christ? And is not the bread that we break a participation in the body of Christ?" (1 Corinthians 10:16). It is a fellowship of sinners redeemed by grace. It is the sweetest fellowship on earth. It is rich in nourishment as together we feed on Christ by faith. By faith we look to the historical Christ represented. As we trust in the sufficiency of his sacrifice, we are nourished. He loves me! He gave himself for me! He is the living Bread who satisfies my deepest hunger and strengthens me to bear fruit for him!

Paul gives a solemn warning to check our attitude toward Christ and others before coming to the Lord's Supper: "Therefore, whoever eats the bread or drinks the cup of the Lord in an unworthy manner will be guilty of sinning against the body and blood of the Lord. A man ought to examine himself before he eats of the bread and drinks of the cup. For anyone who eats and drinks without recognizing the body of the Lord eats and drinks judgment on himself. That is why many among you are weak and sick, and a number of you have fallen asleep. But if we judged ourselves, we would not come under judgment" (1 Corinthians 11:27–31). "It is required of them that would worthily partake of the Lord's Supper, that they examine themselves of their knowledge to discern the Lord's body, of their faith to feed upon him, of their repentance, love, and new obedience; lest, coming unworthily, they eat and drink judgment to themselves" (SC, Q/A 97).

The sacraments of baptism and the Lord's Supper are both means of grace. They are means by which God conveys blessings for our spiritual nourishment and strengthening in grace. As we partake of them by faith, we receive the same kind of blessing as when we hear God's Word preached. The sacraments are the Word in pictures, in signs and seals. To understand their meaning and appropriate the grace promised in them is to receive a blessing. We are not to expect a blessing any different from that which we receive from the preaching of God's Word. We shall, however, receive an additional and very personal blessing. Failure to participate in the sacraments is to rob ourselves of blessing. To rob ourselves is ultimately to injure the body of Christ, because we deprive the body of the ministry that our spiritual growth through the sacraments will bring.

Prayer

There is another important means that God has provided for advancing in grace. That is prayer. Prayer is an indispensable means of growth in grace. Christ, the sinless Savior, was a man of prayer. He would rise a long time before daybreak to pray; he would continue all night in prayer. The hour of his severest trial found him on his knees sweating great drops of blood in agonizing prayer in the Garden of Gethsemane. How then can we, so weak and sinful compared with Christ, be faithful to Christ in *our* trials without the aid of God's grace, obtained through this divinely appointed means?

Prayer is talking to God. Prayer is a living, vital communion of the redeemed sinner with his Lord. "Come near to God and he will come near to you" (James 4:8). As we draw near to God through the blood of the cross, there is a meeting of hearts. We touch the source of all goodness, and respond with love, reverence, thankfulness; we sense peace and blessing. The highest joy that heaven can give to sinful humans is the ability to pray through Christ and in the Spirit, "Abba, Father."

But prayer is essentially more than fellowship with God. It must be that or it is not true prayer. Basically, however, prayer is asking God for things that he has promised to give. Our Lord promised, "If you believe, you will receive whatever you ask for in prayer" (Matthew 21:22). In that case, "let us then approach the throne of grace with confidence, so that we may receive mercy and find grace to help us in our time of need" (Hebrews 4:6).

Are you faced with some besetting sin? "Watch and pray," Jesus warned, "so that you will not fall into temptation" (Mark 14:38). Do you need wisdom for the duties and decisions of the day? "If any of you lacks wisdom," James wrote, "he should ask God, who gives generously to all without finding fault, and it will be given to him" (James 1:5). Do you become weary in doing good, and weak in the face of opposition against you and Christ's church? Our Lord instructed his disciples that they "should always pray and not give up" (Luke 18:1).

Prayer is dealing with God as if he were both willing and "able to do immeasurably more than all we ask or imagine" (Ephesians 3:20). It is believing the sovereignty and grace of God in action. Those who believe in the sovereignty of God should of all people pray the most. We know that he "does as he pleases with the powers of heaven and the peoples of the earth" (Daniel 4:35). Live as if you believed God is both willing and supremely able to do great things for you.

"Prayer is an offering up of our desires unto God, for things agreeable to his will, in the name of Christ, with confession of our sins, and thankful acknowledgment of his mercies" (SC, Q/A 98).

Four important areas to cover in your prayer are:

A—ADORE God. Make his name holy. Declare his majesty.
(Matthew 6:9; Psalm 8:1)

C—CONFESS your sins to God—specifically.
(Psalm 51:2–4; Matthew 6:12, 15)

T—THANK him for his mercies to you, and for his works of creation, providence and salvation.
(Psalm 103:1–5)

S—SUPPLICATE (ask) God to workin your life and in the lives of others; ask him to meet your needs, and to extend and to bring in his kingdom.
(Matthew 6:10, 11, 13)

The first letters of each of these four words spell the word *ACTS*, which can be used as a mental reminder to help you include all these elements in your prayer life.

Fellowship

The Word of God, the sacraments and prayer are provisions of God for our growth in grace. But we must use them in the context of Christian fellowship, which God also provides for our growth. "They devoted themselves to the apostles' teaching and to the *fellowship,* to the breaking of bread and to prayer" (Acts 2:42, emphasis added). We are not just to pray alone, but together as a church, addressing "*Our* Father." We are not just to read the Word of God alone, but to gather in fellowship to hear the Word of God preached publicly. "Let us not give up meeting together, as some are in the habit of doing, but let us encourage one another—and all the more as you see the Day approaching" (Hebrews 10:25).

Throughout the week we must live out our fellowship by encouraging and counseling one another with the truths and promises of God's Word (Romans 15:1–5, 14), and by showing mercy until people's physical needs have been met (Acts 2:45; 4:54). We can easily give up so it is important that we persevere in helping or restoring one another (Galatians 6:1–10; Matthew 18:15–20). As children in God's family, we can only share in this genuine fellowship with one another when we have first been brought into fellowship with the Father through the teaching of the Word of Truth (1 John 1:3, 6, 7). We increasingly come to be more like Christ as we benefit *together* from God's provisions for our development. We live out our common life as his children by sharing ourselves, our homes, and our possessions to meet the needs of others. The Word of God, sacraments and prayer in the context of Christian fellowship are God's ways of giving us the kind of spiritual maturity that leads to a powerful confession of our faith to others (Acts 2:42–47). This confession of our faith to others is the topic of our next and final chapter.

Review Questions (Part 1)

1. What are the God's provisions for our growth in grace?

2. Does the Word of God automatically bring blessing to those who read it? (Hebrews 4:2; 2 Corinthians 2:14–17)

3. How is God's Word to be read and heard so we will be blessed? Give several Bible verses to support your answer.

4. What is a sacrament?

5. Where in the Bible did Jesus command people to be baptized?

6. Are we automatically saved because we are baptized? because we take the Lord's Supper?

7. What does the water of baptism signify?

8. What biblical basis is there for baptizing children of believers?

9. What do we promise when we have our children baptized?

MEMORY WORK
2 Peter 3:18

But grow in the grace and knowledge of our Lord and Savior Jesus Christ. To him be glory both now and forever! Amen. (NIV)

But grow in the grace and knowledge of our Lord and Savior Jesus Christ. To Him be the glory both now and forever. Amen. (NKJV)

Questions for Discussion (Part 1)

1. When do children reach the age of accountability? (Deuteronomy 29:10–13; 1 Corinthians 7:14)

2. Specifically, how can parents keep their promise to teach their children God's Word? (Genesis 18:18, 19; Deuteronomy 6:6–9)

3. How would you answer someone who says that the Bible teaches "repent, believe and be baptized"—and from this concludes that infants are not to be baptized?

Review Questions (Part 2)

1. What do the bread and the wine represent in the Lord's Supper?

2. Of what is the Lord's Supper a seal? Prove it.

3. What is required for partaking worthily of the Lord's Supper?

4. What is the nature of the blessing received in the sacrament of the Lord's Supper?

5. What is prayer?

6. What is the value of prayer?

7. How does God use fellowship to provide for our growth as Christians?

Questions for Discussion (Part 2)

1. What happens if we emphasize or omit one of God's provisions for our growth at the expense of another?

2. What meaning do the sacraments have for Roman Catholic and Lutheran churches?

3. Does it make any difference to whom and through whom we pray, as long as we pray? (John 14:14; 1 John 5:14)

4. What does the Lord's Prayer teach us about prayer? (Matthew 6:9–13)

5. What are the things that prevent our praying as we should?

6. How could sitting at home and reading the Bible instead of assembling with God's people affect a person's Christian growth?

7

CONFESSING CHRIST TO OTHERS

Qualifications and Methods

Confessing Christ involves more than making profession of our Christian faith before the elders and the church. It is partly that. But it is much more. Christ calls upon us to confess him to others. "Therefore whoever confesses me before men, him I will also confess before my Father who is in heaven" (Matthew 10:32—NKJV). In the context, the words "before men" refer to hostile men of the world who persecute those who acknowledge Christ. Receiving Christ places us under obligation to speak of him to others even under difficult circumstances. Paul testified, "I am obligated both to Greeks and non-Greeks, both to the wise and the foolish" (Romans 1:14). We cannot eat our bread alone. We must share the bread of life with others. As beggars who have found bread, we are compelled to tell other beggars where they, too, can find bread.

Before he returned to heaven, Jesus, our Captain, left us with clear marching orders to guide us in the campaign until he returns. "Therefore go and make disciples of all nations, baptizing them in the name of the Father and of the Son and of the Holy Spirit, and teaching them to obey everything I have commanded you. And surely I am with you always, to the very end of the age" (Matthew 28:19, 20). "But you will receive power when the Holy Spirit comes on you; and you will be my witnesses in Jerusalem, and in all Judea and Samaria, and to the ends of the earth" (Acts 1:8).

In following Christ's orders to make disciples throughout the earth, we have the pattern of the early church. When Christians were scattered because of persecution, they "preached the word wherever they went" (Acts 8:4). Every Christian was a witness. This was the strength of the first-century believers. If the church today is to become an effective means of evangelism, each Christian will need to share the gospel with others. Peter set the responsibility for witnessing upon each individual. "Always be prepared," he wrote, "to give an answer to everyone who asks you to give the reason for the hope that you have" (1 Peter 3:15). Christ tells each of us to do what he told the transformed demoniac: "Go home to your family and tell them how much the Lord has done for you, and how he has had mercy on you" (Mark 5:19).

True Christians have a real desire to tell others about Christ. They don't want to deny him by keeping silent. But the difficulties of the task tempt us to say, "I can't." We need to be reminded that the Lord never asks us to do something without equipping us with the knowledge and grace necessary for the task. When the Lord commands, he enables. Whom he calls, he qualifies.

Qualifications

What are the qualifications necessary for confessing Christ to others? They are very simple.

1. Know Christ

We must know certain facts about Jesus and what they mean. Our job is to testify about Christ, not about ourselves. We don't need to know everything the Bible says about Jesus, but we need to know something. For your encouragement, if you know anything at all from the Bible about Christ, you know more than most people today. The minimum that we need to know is that "Christ Jesus came into the world to save sinners—of whom I am the worst" (1 Timothy 1:15). We must know who Jesus is. He is the Christ, the Anointed One, the Messiah; he is Jesus, the Savior. He entered history: was born, lived, died, was buried and rose from the dead. And why? "To save sinners." But knowing the sinfulness of our own hearts, we add, "of whom I am the worst." He died for *our* sins.

Here are a few Scripture verses that pinpoint the way of salvation.

> *Man's need*—Romans 3:23; 6:23
> *God's provision*—John 3:16; Matthew 20:28; 1 Corinthians 15:3
> *God's grace*—Ephesians 2:8, 9
> *God's requirement*— Repent: Luke 13:3; Mark 1:15
> Believe: Acts 16:31

Knowing Christ is more than having accurate information about him. We must know Christ *personally*. Paul testified of his personal relationship to Christ when he wrote, "I have been crucified with Christ and I no longer live, but Christ lives in me. The life I live in the body, I live by faith in the Son of God, who loved *me*... (Galatians 2:20, emphasis added). Paul could say, "I know whom I have believed" (2 Timothy 1:12). We must know what—and whom—we are talking about. Our hearers will soon detect whether or not we do. We must know the redeeming love of Christ in our own lives before we try to tell others about it. Each of us must be able to express what Christ has done for *me* as an individual and what he means to *me*, if only to say simply, as Paul did, "He loved me and gave himself for me." Writing out in your own words how God has worked in your life and why you are trusting Christ, and committing the basics to memory, can be helpful.

2. Live Christ

"By their fruit you will recognize them," Jesus said (Matthew 7:16). Paul wrote of the Corinthians, "You yourselves are our letter...known and read by everybody" (2 Corinthians 3:2). Our lives, as well as our words, are to be a witness to Christ. Others are to see Christ living in us. The fruit of the Spirit is to be obvious in us—"love, joy, peace, patience, kindness, goodness, faithfulness, gentleness and self-control" (Galatians 5:22, 23).

There are many people who were first attracted to Christ by the lives of Christians they knew. For example, it was the beauty of holiness in young Robert McCheyne (a 17th-century Scottish minister) that first attracted an observer to want to learn of Christ. An ill-tempered policeman in Japan regularly noticed a man who never lost his temper, learned that he was a Christian, and then sought and found Christ as his Savior and Lord. A woman asks her Christian friend, "Why are you always so happy?"—and the door opens wide for witnessing to Christ. A rebellious son finally gives in to the godly life of his mother and believes in her Savior. An unbelieving daughter sees the joy of the Lord in her father who is suffering and dying from cancer and longs that her father's Savior might become hers. The Holy Spirit uses our lives in Christ to gain a hearing for the gospel. Unless we adorn the gospel with godliness, however, we may repel people. Our lives can become barriers to their becoming Christians.

3. Love People

Loving people means seeing them as God's creatures. "Love your neighbor as yourself" (Matthew 22:39). "Do good to all people" (Galatians 6:10). "Rejoice with those who rejoice; mourn with those who mourn" (Romans 12:15). Loving people means being involved in the lives of our daily associates at work, at school, or in the neighborhood. Love involves communicating our concern in word and in deed. We should seek to *be* friends not just to *have* friends. To be a friend takes thought and time; it means giving ourselves. Whenever evangelistic services are held by your church, the ones most likely to respond to an invitation to attend will be those who have been befriended by the Christian who invites them.

We love people even though they, like us, are sinners. "He [Jesus] had compassion on them, because they were like sheep without a shepherd" (Mark 6:34). Christ saw people as lost sheep that needed to come back to the Father's fold. He didn't remain aloof from people but was known as "a friend of tax collectors and 'sinners' " (Matthew 11:19)—gougers of the poor and notorious adulterers. While Christ didn't approve of their sins, he accepted these people just as they were.

Often we can't get past the things in other people that repel us. We tend to forget that while we ourselves were still sinners, Christ died for us. He loved us as we were; we should love people as they are. A world traveler was once asked what was the most beautiful sight he had seen in all his travels. He responded, "It was seeing Borden of Yale [a Phi Beta Kappa and a millionaire] with his arm around a bum in the Yale Hope Mission." We must be able to put a loving arm around a person in need and show him the Great Physician, who delights in healing those sick with the humanly incurable disease called sin (Luke 5:30–32).

Methods

"But how do I start confessing Christ to others? How do I go about it?" Begin with prayer. Pray that God will open doors of opportunity. Seize the opportunities that God provides in answer to your prayers. Pray for courage to speak boldly when the doors open, because each opening to speak of Christ brings the temptation not to witness but to speak of everything except Christ (Colossians 4:2–6).

We need to pray unceasingly for ourselves. We need to pray, too, for our hearers. Only the Spirit of God can open eyes to see and hearts to receive Christ. People's eyes are spiritually blind and their hearts are hard as stone. Much as we would like to change people spiritually, we can't. But the Holy Spirit can and does. Christ has promised, "If you then, though you are evil, know how to give good gifts to your children, how much more will your Father in heaven give the Holy Spirit to those who ask him!" (Luke 11:13). Ask!

1. Bible Study

One effective way of witnessing to others is through a program of Bible study. Philip the evangelist used this method in his encounter with the Ethiopian eunuch (Acts 8:26–39). Many people today have never had occasion to study the Bible and would appreciate such an opportunity. This may be done one-on-one or in a group. Your pastor will be able to suggest something suitable to the needs of those with whom you would like to have a Bible study. Either the Gospel of John or the First Epistle of John is excellent for those just beginning to study the Bible.

2. Personal Witnessing

More important than *how* we witness is *that* we witness. Any witness to Christ given in love is better than no witness at all. Some find it so difficult to make any approach—to say even the first word—that they say nothing. This is to deny Christ by silence.

Our testimony to others will vary according to the personality and circumstances of the person we speak to. "Let your conversation be always full of grace, seasoned with salt, so that you may know how to answer everyone" (Colossians 4:6). Determining how we should relate to the listener is important to being effective. Since Jesus was the greatest interpersonal communicator of all, his methods are worth examining.

Basically, Christ used two different approaches in his personal contacts: one was gradual, step-by-step; the other was a swift, immediate confrontation.

The step-by-step approach is superbly illustrated in our Lord's conversation with the woman of Samaria at the well (John 4:5–29). First, he simply asked for a drink of water—a very natural and appropriate request. But in requesting a drink he was actually, and surprisingly, demonstrating his love for the woman, which she recognized in her response: " 'You are a Jew and I am a Samaritan woman. How can you ask me for a drink?' (For Jews do not associate with Samaritans.)" (John 4:9). Jesus then turned the conversation around to her thirst for spiritual water, which produces eternal life (vss. 13–15).

Next he exposed her sin of adultery. He confronted her with the fact that she had had five husbands and that the man she was now living with was not her husband (vss. 16–18). Then Jesus dealt with her question of where to worship (vss. 20–23). Finally, he presented himself as the Messiah. "The woman said, 'I know that Messiah' (called Christ) 'is coming. When he comes, he will explain everything to us.' Then Jesus declared, 'I who speak to you am he' " (vss. 25, 26). The woman believed and immediately began to tell others of Christ. Slowly, deliberately, Jesus answered her questions, and brought her to see her need, her sin and her Savior. We must cultivate the love, the wisdom and the patience to do as he did.

At other times Christ moved swiftly to confront others with specific problems and their solutions. To Nicodemus, a ruler of the Jews who came under cover of darkness to interview him, Jesus said abruptly and pointedly, "I tell you the truth, no one can see the kingdom of God unless he is born again" (John 3:3).

This method, too, was blessed of the Spirit. Later chapters show that Nicodemus courageously spoke out against those who unjustly condemned Christ and finally, at considerable cost, helped Joseph of Arimathea prepare the body of Jesus for burial (John 7:50–52; 19:39–42). On another occasion, when the rich young ruler asked Jesus for the way to eternal life, our Lord quickly probed to the heart of the young man. He saw the idol of riches in the man's heart and laid before him the absolute necessity of repentance and faith. "One thing you lack," he said, "Go, sell everything you have and give to the poor, and you will have treasure in heaven. Then come, follow me" (Mark 10:21).

How can we use this direct method today? There are several pairs of direct questions we can ask as we talk with non-Christians.

- Are you a Christian?
- What do you think a Christian is?

- Have you reached the point in your life where you are sure your sins are forgiven and you have eternal life?
- What is the basis of your assurance?

- If you die tonight, do you think you would go to heaven?
- On what basis do you think God would receive you?

We need much wisdom in deciding which method is better in a given situation—the gradual approach or the instant confrontation. In either case, we have to get to the point and confront the sinner with his need and with the Savior's redeeming grace. And remember, almost anything we say in love will be better than saying nothing at all.

Remember too, personal witnessing should be interwoven with an entire life of faithfully contending for Christ. "Contend for the faith that was once for all entrusted to the saints" (Jude 3). "Fight the good fight of the faith. Take hold of the eternal life to which you were called when you made your good confession in the presence of many witnesses. In the sight of God, who gives life to everything, and of Christ Jesus, who while testifying before Pontius Pilate made the good confession, I charge you to keep this command without spot or blame until the appearing of our Lord Jesus Christ" (1 Timothy 6:12–14).

Though we face opposition, Christ is already the victor. He is our risen Lord and captain. While we wait for his return, we are to be faithful confessors, sturdy contenders, joyous soldiers, who uphold the glorious gospel of his kingdom in our entire life and witness. Our goal is to glorify Christ, build his church and bring others to know the joy of serving under his banner.

Review Questions

1. How do we know that all Christians are supposed to confess Christ to others?

2. What is the minimum we have to know about Christ in order to share our faith with others? (1 Timothy 1:15)

3. Is it enough just to know facts about Christ? In what other way must we know him?

4. How important to confessing Christ is the life we live? Why? (John 13:35)

5. How will our love toward others be obvious?

6. What should we pray for as we seek to witness to others?

7. How can Bible studies be used to lead others to Christ?

8. What was Christ's approach to the woman of Samaria?

9. What was Christ's approach to Nicodemus?

10. What are some good questions to ask those we are witnessing to?

11. What is worse than making a mistake in the way we talk to people about Christ?

MEMORY WORK
1 Peter 3:15

But in your hearts set apart Christ as Lord. Always be prepared to give an answer to everyone who asks you to give the reason for the hope that you have. But do this with gentleness and respect. (NIV)

But sanctify the Lord God in your hearts, and always be ready to give a defense to everyone who asks you a reason for the hope that is in you, with meekness and fear. (NKJV)

Questions for Discussion

1. What things keep us from confessing Christ to others as we should? How can these be overcome?

2. How can tracts and books best be used to lead others to Christ?

3. How much effort is one soul worth? (Luke 15:4)

4. How can our good-neighbor policy lead people to Christ?

5. How does the teaching of God's electing love in Christ (Ephesians 1:4, 5) encourage us in confessing Christ to others? (Acts 18:10; 2 Timothy 2:9, 10)

6. How does knowing that God must first work in a person's life before that person will change affect our attitude in witnessing? (2 Timothy 2:24–26)

7. Did Christ approach people by first telling them "God loves you and has a wonderful plan for your life" or by confronting them with their sin and need of the Savior? Give proof from Scripture.

8. How can sharing our personal testimony enhance our witness?

9. What responsibility do we have to confess Christ to other nations? How can we as Christ's church fulfill this responsibility?